Fore
Forensic Neurops)

DECEIVED
AN INVESTIGATIVE MEMOIR OF THE
ZION SOCIETY CULT

Michael R. King

Profiling Evil, LLC
www.ProfilingEvil.com
ProfilingEvil@gmail.com
USA

Published 2021 by Profiling Evil, LLC

For permission contact the publisher at:
Profiling Evil, LLC • ProfilingEvil@gmail.com
ProfilingEvil.com

Cover design by Circa3, Tyler Cahoon and Scott Wiser.
Cover photo of hands by Jeremy Bishop on Unsplash.

ISBN (Hardcover): 978-1-7362374-0-3
ISBN (Paperback): 978-1-7362374-1-0

Dedication

This book is dedicated to victims of child sexual abuse whose voices are often silenced; and to those who believe, defend, and protect them. It is also dedicated to anyone who has experienced destructive mind control and has found the strength to remove themselves from it.

CONTENTS

v

Foreword
by Dr. Judy Ho

So many stories of chance connection with amazing people nowadays happen through social media, and this one is no different. I woke up one morning to find an intriguing email in my inbox with an invitation to join Mike King on his popular Profiling Evil YouTube show. A quick journey down Google over my morning coffee revealed Mike's phenomenal contribution to law enforcement which has spanned over four decades with numerous accolades and achievements in federal, state, and local jurisdictions. As I viewed a few recent episodes of Profiling Evil, I became increasingly excited to be a guest on his program. I am continually fascinated with the process of criminal investigation and profiling as a board certified clinical and forensic neuropsychologist and have come across many investigators who have made it their life's work to root out and prosecute criminals in my professional work. But Mike really stood out to me as heads above the rest in so many ways. Incredible achievements aside, he really seemed to have a deep understanding of the psychological underpinnings of both criminals and victims, and a keen ability to utilize both the analytical and creative parts of his mind in his investigations in order to accomplish his objectives.

Mike is so thoughtful in his analyses and clearly demonstrates his expertise, but he is also such a brilliant storyteller. Observing Mike's jovial communication style and bright personality on screen, I wondered how he was able to do the extremely difficult work of investigating the myriad of complex and horrific crimes over the course of his career and still emerge on the other side full of humor, empathy, and kindness. It would come as no surprise that I pushed for a theme of "Psychology of a Police Investigation" for my guest appearance on Profiling Evil. While I was grateful for the forum to contribute my professional expertise on his show, I wanted to more deeply understand the psychological underpinnings of Mike's everyday work as an investigator from beginning to end. I joked with Mike that I wanted to analyze him! Specifically, how does a skilled investigator like Mike prepare for his investigations? What does it take to get the straight story out of witnesses? How can you assess someone's likely traits and potential behaviors before they even speak a word? How do you put the breadcrumbs together into a coherent whole and discover the truth once and for all when others have failed? And after a case is adjudicated – what happens to the victims and their families as they grapple with their trauma and memories, even after justice was served?

As a board certified clinical and forensic neuropsychologist, I am often retained as an expert witness on both civil and criminal cases and asked to provide my psychological expertise on a variety of TV programs, podcasts, and print/electronic articles. With the advent of the true crime takeover in this last decade, I have been increasingly called upon to analyze the "why's" and "how's" of a crime. Everyone wants to know how heinous crimes could potentially occur in their wholesome, tight-knit communities; how a seemingly innocuous, charming, and lovely person could turn out to be a serial murderer; and how they might avoid such tragedies from happening to themselves and their family members. Over the years, I've analyzed the psychological profiles of history's most notorious criminals including Ted Bundy, Jeffrey Dahmer, and John Wayne Gacy to those of recent criminals still making headlines today. I've met with and assessed individuals charged with horrific deeds, and in my role as expert witness, presented my analyses to the court so that the jury and judge can make important decisions about what to do with these individuals. Do they deserve a second chance? Did they understand the crimes they allegedly committed? And could they ever become rehabilitated into productive, contributing members of society, or are they just…evil?

One of the specialty areas I've often been asked to opine about is how humans can be prone to groupthink and even be brainwashed, made to act against their better judgment to the point of cutting out loved ones, participating in abusive behaviors, and committing increasingly atrocious crimes – and having some way of justifying these unthinkable actions to themselves. This mostly comes up in the context of cults, and I've given many lectures and spoken on various TV programs about how intelligent, well-meaning, and kind individuals can fall prey to such groups. While there isn't a universal psychological profile of people who end up affiliating with cults, some common characteristics emerge. Namely, these individuals are seeking purpose and looking for a community who loves and cares for them. They want to dedicate themselves to a cause greater than themselves and have aspirations of doing something amazing with their lives and for society at large. Cult leaders take advantage of these individuals and corrupt their hopes and dreams. Through a variety of systematic techniques, these cult leaders' charm, isolate, and indoctrinate their recruits and normalize their extremist and often abusive ideologies to them, obtaining unquestioned obedience over time.

When Mike asked me to contribute the foreword to his new book, "Deceived: An investigative memoir of the Zion Society cult," I was honored and delighted for the opportunity because of my own fascination with cults through my professional work, but also because I would have a chance to get an up-close look at how Mike investigates a case from beginning to end. His exemplary work in this investigation led to the ultimate take-down of a deviant polygamous cult, whose leader propagated some of the most repugnant, violent crimes against women and children and indoctrinated his followers into doomsday beliefs that kept them obeying his every command out of fear. You will get to witness the anatomy of an investigation through Mike's eyes and be taken into a secret world through the accounts of his witnesses that will keep you turning the pages because you can't wait to learn what will happen next. Each reveal is more shocking than the last, and despite the mayhem and chaos, Mike expertly pieces together the ultimate puzzle of an extremely complex case involving many players and layers who through deliberate thought and action concocted an intricate web of deceit and lies that preyed on the most vulnerable and kind of our society. This brilliant investigative memoir will give you a behind-the-scenes look into how Mike, as the lead investigator, played an integral role to gathering the hard-to-find evidence that was crucial for serving justice. Mike's work directly resulted in the rescue of 32 children and the conviction of 12 cult members who were all convicted of their crimes of sexual assault.

This book has it all – intellectually scintillating deep dives into the investigation for the true crime buffs, relatable character portrayals of people who joined the cult looking for love and community, and heartwarming stories of hope and redemption after trauma. Mike is an expert author, having penned several books in his illustrious career, and this latest volume is one you won't be able to put down. It is a book you'll want to tell your friends about; a book that will leave a lasting impression with you long after you've finished it. What stuck with me most is how this book demonstrates Mike's expertise, compassion, and unwavering diligence in his investigative approach; he forged forward no matter how difficult the case details became until the victims were rescued and their cases heard. And he didn't stop there. In the past three decades, he continued to follow members of the cult as they were released after serving their time to track their whereabouts. Even more remarkably, he kept in touch with the victims, culminating in the incredible moment they reconnected as adults to recount their experiences, celebrate their triumph over trauma, and to applaud

Mike's efforts for helping them to reintegrate into society and find new lives. At the core, this book is a story about hope and resiliency, and how some of the most beautiful human stories can emerge from extreme darkness and pain.

Dr. Judy Ho
Clinical and Forensic Neuropsychologist
Associate Professor at Pepperdine University
Author, *Stop Self-Sabotage*

Author's Note

Some stories are hard to read, let alone write. It doesn't mean they should not be told. This book is one of those stories. This memoir chronicles my investigation into a deviant religious cult of child sex abuse. To ignore, avoid, or pretend such events do not occur is not helpful to victims, potential victims, or society in general. Awareness is the first step to healing and protecting victims, and ultimately bringing perpetrators to justice. Extreme details of this case have been left out. All that is important to know is that the events happened.

. . .

(The information in this book was gathered from my own memories and case notes, and the recollections of many others who were involved with the case. Some names have been changed or left out for various reasons.)

I can think of no more important book at this moment in our history than Deceived: An Investigative Memoir of the Zion Society Cult. Mike King has made a superb and vitally important contribution by exposing the abuse of women and children in that heinous cult. And this still happens far too often in the multitude of harmful groups around the world. If you want to understand coercive influence and control, then read this book.

Janja Lalich
Ph.D. Professor Emerita of Sociology
Cult Educator and Author of *Escaping Utopia*

Prologue

In the next few years, this earth will be rocked and buffeted by the most fearful destruction in the history of mankind. Millions shall perish. Suffering beyond human imaginations will occur, and all the prophesied plagues, diseases, earthquakes, floods, wars, and pestilence of every imaginable kind will be poured out without measure. Men shall wish to die to escape the horror of it all. I cannot paint in words, even a millionth part of the death and horror that awaits this generation.

This dire warning from a self-proclaimed prophet of God was designed to strike fear into the hearts of his gullible followers. For more than a decade, the leader of the Zion Society cult wielded complete control over his devotees. They viewed themselves as the spiritually elite. They had come from near and far seeking the exclusive communications of God's will that their leader promised to provide. Some came to practice polygamy secretly, which they believed was sanctioned by God.

This so-called prophet spoke to his followers in language reminiscent of scripture, and cult members fell for his lies. In his soft-spoken way, he demanded their complete allegiance and devotion.

Once followers experienced sufficient angst from his repeated threats and intimidations, the leader would offer hope.

A special blessing of protection in the last days will encircle those who would bring forth plural marriage and Sister Councils. It is a promise that they would be protected and delivered from the vengeance of God and the cleansing of the earth. Yes, those who embark upon such programs will not taste the bitter wrath of God when it is poured out without measure upon the earth.

The grandfatherly leader who prided himself in his gardening skills was persuasive and manipulative. But he was no man of God. He was a con man, a narcissist, a sex pervert, and a pedophile. He had spent years concocting his abominable "religion" as a guise to satisfy his many perversions. With his abhorrent program called Sister Councils, he managed to convince members of his cult to participate in some of the most repugnant crimes against women and children ever seen in the state of Utah. If not for the courage of a young woman who had been recruited into the cult, the horrible practices might never have been discovered.

We know that people can be led to buy almost anything.... In addition to buying almost anything, people can apparently be led to believe almost anything.... Cults know that if you knew from the get-go what you were in for and why, you would never join. It's as simple as that.

Singer, Margaret Thaler, with Lalich, Janja (2003)
Cults in our Midst, Jossey-Bass

PART ONE

"I didn't go there to join a cult; I went
there to escape a bad marriage."
                                    Erin Anderson

1

The Confession

July 10, 1991

I heard my office phone ringing down the hall as I stepped out of the municipal building elevator. My workday seemed to be starting without me. As an investigator in the county attorney's office assigned to work property crimes, my days were never quiet. A relentless backload of cases stacked up daily. I rushed to my seventh-floor office only to find I had missed the call. Taking advantage of a quiet moment, I sat down at my desk and began preparations for an upcoming STING operation.

My office was generally a hive of activity and today would be no different. It wasn't long before investigators started filing in and out and the phone began again. I ignored it, hoping the receptionist would take a message. The incessant ringing became increasingly annoying, so I grabbed the receiver and abruptly answered, "This is King." The caller on the other end was our office receptionist asking me to come to the lobby to meet someone.

Another interruption to my already busy day.

Impatiently, I stepped into the lobby. The receptionist gestured toward a young woman seated in a chair.

"Mike, this woman has been waiting to talk to someone for a while—can you help her?"

The woman appeared to be in her twenties and very petite. She was attractive and well-dressed all in black. Her hair was also black, big and stiff with hairspray. She wore plenty of makeup. It was clear she had spent a lot of time getting ready for the day. She looked up from the magazine she was flipping through and politely stood to greet me.

"My name is Erin Anderson," she said with a very slight lisp. "I need to talk to someone about a cult I have been a member of that is sexually abusing children. Do you have time to talk to me?"

The air seemed to leave the room.

Did I hear her correctly? Did this woman just confess to sexually abusing children?

I stood stunned, frozen. This was the last thing I expected to hear today especially from such a successful looking young woman. She spoke so matter-of-factly that I was caught off guard. I had handled confessions before; this was not the first, nor would it be the last. But usually, confessions came with carefully planned interviews and often times just plain luck. Rarely, did someone offer one without some sort of provocation. *

"Sure," I said as calmly and professionally as possible, "why don't we step into my office?"

I tried to gather my thoughts as we walked through my office door. I pulled up a chair and invited the young woman to sit down. Before I could say anything, she blurted out what seemed to be a rehearsed statement.

There are documented accounts by the "The Innocence Project," (a team of criminal justice professionals who have exonerated hundreds of wrongly convicted people through DNA testing), that show incidents of people confessing to things they didn't do, resulting in prison sentences. Their findings suggest that one fourth of those inmates who were exonerated had actually made false confessions to the crimes they were convicted of and the reasons for the confession varied. Some confessed because of real or perceived intimidation, devious interrogation techniques or fear. For some reason, most people will ultimately agree to a police interview when asked. Some experts suggest that it is their way of ensuring police that they are innocent of any charges. Fortunately, law enforcement officers have a much better chance of extracting the truth from people when they can talk to them shortly after a crime, rather than having to filter the information which becomes orchestrated or contaminated over time. With Erin, her initial 4-hour confession would come three months after the last criminal act she committed.

"I came to the county attorney's office because of the guilt I have been feeling for a long time. I know terrible crimes are being committed. I need to remove this heavy burden and turn the abusers in."

"Hold on," I said. "First, I would like to get some personal information from you."

She took a deep breath, seemingly relieved.

I wanted to make sure the interview, which could turn into an interrogation, was legal and had structure. I pointed to the locations of the restrooms and the exits.

"Remember, you can leave at any time," I said.

I reached for an old vintage cassette recorder I kept on a dusty shelf and told her I would be recording our conversation. I then pulled a Miranda Rights card from my desk drawer. Although I knew the warning by heart, I wanted to make sure everything was done by the book. I pushed the record button and began reading Erin her rights.

"You have the right to remain silent......" I read. "Do you understand each of these rights I have explained to you?"

"Yes, I do," she said without hesitation.

Erin then began the interview with one of the most captivating statements I had heard in my career.

"Until a few months ago, I was a member of the Zion Society."

No sooner did the words leave her mouth than I interrupted, "Can you repeat that? A member of what?"

Patiently, she repeated, "I was a member of the Zion Society."

I had heard her correctly. I was actually interviewing someone from a secretive, religious cult in a housing development called the Northwood Subdivision that the police department had heard rumors about for some time.

For several years, there was talk around the city that a group of religious zealots had formed their own religion. There were allegations that the group was practicing polygamy, but no credible evidence had ever surfaced to support the claims. Almost an urban legend of sorts, the sect had been the topic of behind-doors gossip and intrigue for nearly a decade.

Rumors had it that the group was purchasing several small homes in the northern Ogden, Utah neighborhood. Oddly, elaborately landscaped yards distinguished cult members' houses from those belonging to their neighbors. It wasn't uncommon for neighbors to report carloads of onlookers cruising the quiet streets to see the beautiful yards and perhaps catch a glimpse of the homeowners. Some neighbors resorted to placing signs on their front lawns that read: *We are not one of them!*

Access into the neighborhood was only possible through one street. This led to speculation that cult members surveilled each vehicle and pedestrian who entered and reported such movement to the group's leaders.

Curious myself, I had personally driven through the neighborhood dozens of times looking for anything to substantiate these rumors. Within a few minutes of interviewing, Erin had.

As I listened, it became apparent that the existence of a religious cult in Ogden was only the tip of the iceberg. Without hesitation, Erin went on to explain the group was led by a 61-year-old man named Arvin. Ironically, along with many gardens around the city, Arvin was credited with designing and maintaining the famous Ogden City Municipal Gardens surrounding the police department. Nearly every city official knew him.

Arvin, Erin added, had already recruited over 100 followers who considered him to be a prophet of God. He proclaimed to have godly authority to direct and control the group members' daily affairs including all aspects of finances, education, religion, and even individual sexuality. She said he preached that he had received instructions from God to take multiple wives of all ages, including little girls. Erin went on to say Arvin eventually coerced the members of his group to engage in an abhorrent program he claimed was sanctioned by God that consisted of deviant sexual practices involving children.

"I want you to know that I didn't go there to become a member of a cult; I went there to escape a bad marriage," she said, her voice trembling.

I was both horrified and stunned. If these appalling accusations were true, we would be dealing with what was likely the biggest and most significant child sex abuse case in the history of the state if not the country.

After what seemed like a few minutes, I glanced at the wall clock and was surprised to see that more than three hours had passed since Erin had begun talking. We were both emotionally exhausted and I suggested we take a break, that perhaps it would make better sense to regroup the following day. She breathed a sigh of what appeared to be relief.

As Erin stood to leave, she glanced around. She paused to view some photographs of my family I had placed about the office.

"Your children are beautiful," she said and then grew silent for a moment. "They look safe. That's something I denied my daughter." Tears welled up in her eyes.

After she'd gone, I found myself feeling considerable sorrow for this young woman despite what she had just revealed. If the things she had said were true, I worried she might very well, out of self-preservation, change her mind and not return for our appointment scheduled for the next morning. I also couldn't help wondering if there might be some hidden motivations for her confession. Did she have a secret agenda?

I immediately slipped into county attorney Reed Richards' office to brief him on this explosive interview. I had joined the prosecutor's office four years earlier at the young age of 27, shortly after local defense attorney Richards was elected as the new county attorney.

Although I had grown up in Salt Lake City, I began my law enforcement career in a small department outside of Ogden. I quickly moved on to the Ogden Police Department where I developed my love for police work. The rush of adrenaline when responding to a violent crime in progress was exciting. Every call was different, and you needed to think quickly in order to be successful.

I came to know Richards when I was a young patrol officer and we faced one another in the district court. He was defending a woman named Kitty Eakes who was charged with pre-meditated murder and I was one of the prosecution's key witnesses. Months earlier, Eakes had killed her lover's wife, Sharon Wetzel, in a pre-meditated, execution-style shooting. Hours after the murder, Eakes had approached me as I sat in my squad car in a nearby park and said she wanted to confess to the killing. After declining her Miranda rights, she provided a full confession during a formal interrogation. Following her confession, and just moments before being booked into the Weber County Jail, she asked if I could make a phone call to her attorney to let him know what happened. It was nearly midnight, but I made the call to Richards at his home. When I told him what his client had confessed to, he ordered, "Tell her not to answer any questions." I readily complied.

In the months that followed, Richards and I exchanged warm "jabs" at each other as the case progressed through the court system, eventually ending with a guilty plea by Eakes. I remember standing in the back of the courtroom as she was led away by the sheriff's deputies, thinking there are no winners in most criminal cases. Richards and I just happened to exit the courtroom at the same time. He turned to me and said, "We had no choice. She clearly confessed to the crime and since every judge in the county thinks you can't tell a lie, we didn't have a chance. All you have to do is smile with that baby face and those dimples and you win your cases." *I'll take it as a compliment, but I've always hated being called a baby face.* A few months later, when Richards was elected Weber County Attorney, he asked me to join his office. Later he told me that he offered me the job because of my performance in the Eakes case.

Friendly and extroverted, the forty-three-year-old Richards came across as easy-going, but he had the unique ability to get you to do things out of your comfort zone. One of the first things I noticed about him was his signature laugh. Like his professional dealings, it was short, decisive, and to the point—one big, loud "Ha." He was average height and weight and as long as I knew him, he kept a deep side part in his chestnut-colored hair. As well as being an outdoorsman and heavily involved in scouting, he was also deeply religious and served in leadership positions in his church. Although he had a jovial smile and appeared casual in his manner, as an attorney, Richards spoke deliberately and intelligently.

After providing him with a detailed overview of the case's emerging facts, I expressed my concern as to whether Erin was telling the truth.

"She seems very sincere," I said. "But the allegations are so bizarre and horrific. They are just incredibly hard to believe. I also wonder what has motivated her to turn herself in."

As we talked through every detail Erin had shared, we came to the agreement that an immediate and in-depth investigation was warranted in order to better understand the complaint. "If these allegations are true," said Richards, "the children have to be protected."

My first order of business was to look into this so-called prophet.

2
Self-proclaimed

Arvin was born in a middle-class neighborhood in central Ogden in 1930. The city, with a population of nearly 90,000, is located 35 miles north of Salt Lake City. It is beautifully nestled between the Great Salt Lake and the Wasatch Mountain Range and lies in the shadow of Mount Ben Lomond, a 9,700-foot mountain peak.

Ogden has a rich history of contrasts. The community was first established around 1844 by trapper Miles Goodyear and later named after trapper Peter Skene Ogden. Mormon pioneers entered the Utah territory in 1847. And in 1851, the president of the Church of Jesus Christ of Latter-day Saints, Brigham Young, sent "Mormon" pioneer, church leader, and polygamist, Lorin Farr, to the new settlement to be its first mayor. As Ogden grew, religion became the bedrock of the community and churches began to dot every part of the town. Each Sunday, businesses closed their doors, while churches flung theirs wide open. The pews filled up with folks who came dressed in their Sunday best to sing hymns, listen to sermons, and visit with neighbors.

Church also dominated the community's social life with frequent musical programs, dinners, and picnics. Each year on July 24th, Ogden's citizens celebrated the pioneers' 1847 entrance into the territory with rodeos, parades, and pageantry. For many years, most of the residents were acquainted with each other or even related in some distant way. As time passed, the community of mostly very conservative Latter-day Saints (formerly known as Mormons) began growing and experiencing economic success. Many successful businesses, including John Browning's gun manufacturing company, were established and farms flourished, irrigated by two rivers.

Similar to other towns in the state, Ogden was a rather quiet community. That changed in 1869 when the transcontinental railroad was completed north of the city, connecting the eastern United States with the west coast. Much to the disappointment of Utah's capital city, Ogden was delighted to be chosen as the junction for the Union Pacific and Central Pacific railways. The Union Pacific built a large station at the bottom of the city's 25th street just west of the city center leaving it bustling with vast numbers of travelers for many years. The trains brought much-welcome commerce and development to the growing town, but they also brought an unwanted element. Travelers from all walks of life frequented the city streets as they passed through and some had notorious backgrounds. During prohibition days, 25th street became infamous as speakeasies and brothels popped up along the thoroughfare. Rumors began to spread about secret opium dens operating in the basements of some buildings lining the street. One rumor had it that Al Capone traveled to Ogden in the 1920s, but once he walked down 25th Street, he turned around and headed back to the train station admitting the town was too rough, even for him. The police department had its hands full dealing with this district. For decades, nearly every citizen of Ogden avoided 25th Street.

In 1940, Ogden's historic municipal building was completed. Impressive in appearance and built in the Art Deco style, the twelve-story high landmark perched on the corner of the notorious 25th Street and Washington Boulevard, the main street of downtown. The building housed the police department and city and county offices. It was hoped the building's proximity to the seedy district would help to deter crime in the area. It would take decades for Ogden's 25th Street to transform from its disreputable roots into a trendy neighborhood of shops and restaurants housed in historic buildings.

It was during the height of Ogden's contradictions that Arvin was born and raised. He was a very neat and clean-cut young man who was shy and reserved.[1] He once confided to a friend that he had been sexually assaulted by an aunt several times, adding that he enjoyed the encounters, nonetheless. Arvin's family eventually moved to a small suburb of Ogden, where he attended Weber High School. An excellent student, Arvin blossomed in high school debate classes. He developed his natural persuasive ability and would use it to manipulate those around him, eventually winning the coveted position of student body president. He had the uncanny ability to garner respect from the students whenever he spoke.[2] He also served on the Latter-day Saint seminary council at the school. Arvin's success in high school culminated when he captured the state championship in debate. Following graduation, Arvin attended Weber College in Ogden where he also excelled in debate. He would take second place in a competition at the school with his topic, "Resolved, that the federal government should provide a complete system of medical care available to all citizens at public expense." He also took first place in the oratory category of the competition.[3]

Like most people in the community, Arvin was raised in a religious family and worshiped in a local unit of the Church of Jesus Christ of Latter-day Saints. Religion was the center of the family's life. In keeping with the Church's tradition of sending young men to serve full-time missions, he accepted an assignment to proselytize for three years in Brazil and Uruguay. He left in November of 1950 and after he returned home, he was married in September of 1953.[4] Within a few months of marrying, he found employment in the county and city parks department where he worked faithfully until his retirement. He is credited with designing many of the beautiful parks and gardens around Ogden City and was well known in the community as a talented and creative landscaper. It was a standing joke that, "Arvin could make dirt turn green!"

Arvin was very active in his church and became a popular Sunday school teacher, applying the skills he had developed in debate and public speaking to the lessons he taught. His classes were a favorite of many people in the local congregation and beyond. At their request, he began a religious study group held during the week, an activity that was not sponsored by his church. Arvin's classes became so popular, the church hall would fill to overflowing. Thrilled with the attention he received, Arvin used these weeknight classes to introduce ideas he had been having about plural marriage.

Plural marriage, or polygamy, once practiced by some in the Latter-day Saint church, was not legal at that time in Utah or the United States and was firmly declared against the teachings of the Church by 1890. The Church continues to repudiate the practice of polygamy and any derivative groups that practice it.*

In 1990, polygamy was still illegal in Utah and across the United States; cohabitation however was not. In Utah, law enforcement usually turned a blind eye to the practice. Most groups were peaceable and non-threatening. When illegal activities such as tax evasions and child brides were discovered, the law moved in and made arrests. Polygamy in Utah was decriminalized in 2020.

Arvin had studied the issue of polygamy extensively and felt that he should educate others in the practice. As he ramped up his enthusiasm in teaching the subject in his weeknight study groups, some in attendance became so uncomfortable with his ideas that they reported him to their local ecclesiastic leader, a bishop.

Soon, Arvin received an invitation to meet with the bishop and explain his controversial actions. The bishop questioned Arvin about

---

* There are estimated to be nearly 50,000 polygamists in the U.S. In the early 1840's, plural marriage, or polygamy, was introduced to members of the Church of Jesus Christ of Latter-day Saints (formerly called Mormons) by their prophet, Joseph Smith, as he sought to restore ancient principles practiced in the Old Testament. Some members began practicing the principle but in 1862 after Mormon pioneers fled to the Salt Lake Valley to avoid persecution, the U.S. government passed laws against the practice. In 1890 the Church declared its intention to submit to the law. In 1904 the church officially declared that those entering into plural marriage would be excommunicated.[5] This was challenging for the families that had been practicing polygamists and some chose to continue with the practice even if they were excommunicated. This created "generational" polygamy, and the practice continued in small numbers through the years.

the plural marriage doctrine he was promoting and reminded him sternly that it was not in line with the Church's teachings. Without any kind of warning, Arvin boldly declared he had received a revelation from God about the ancient practice and that he had been instructed by God to re-institute it in a specialized form. Aghast, the bishop told him to discontinue the lessons and his claim to divine authority immediately or risk church discipline. Realizing his church membership was in jeopardy, Arvin pretended humility and assured the bishop he would comply. Secretly, however, he continued to share his ideas with those who attended his home study classes or with any audience that would listen.

Little did his bishop know at the time, when Arvin wasn't busy teaching Sunday school or holding his secret weekly religion classes, he was actively soliciting sex workers in Salt Lake City. One of the women he regularly contacted was Melanie.

"He was so kind and gentle, and he reminded me of a bad Mr. Roger's figure," she said. "He was not profane and never swore. He had a soft, gentle voice and appeared to always have a happy smirk on his face," she recalled after remembering at least ten encounters with him.

At one point, Arvin asked Melanie to make arrangements for him to have sex with young girls. She complied on one occasion and set him up with a 16-year-old runaway who was "turning tricks" to make ends meet. On another occasion, he asked if he could be with her young daughter and when she refused, he asked, "How about some 14-year-old girls?" One of Arvin's secret meetings with Melanie resulted in an arrest by the Salt Lake City Police Department VICE Squad.

At home, Arvin excused his actions by telling his wife, Alice, "God has instructed me to experiment with the prostitutes. I don't want to do this, but I cannot offend God." Alice acquiesced and remained silent about the subject.

Word that Arvin was continuing his lectures on polygamy once again reached his bishop who, for a second time, admonished him to stop. Undeterred, and even appearing annoyed with the meddling, Arvin continued to argue with clergy about his disregard of church counsel. As he walked this personal tightrope between his actions and the counsel from his church leaders, his local clergy prepared to hold a church disciplinary council on him.

One evening, in the early 1960s, Arvin was asked to come to the church and meet with local church leaders who oversaw the region where he attended services. With Arvin present, the leaders reviewed his refusal to discontinue teaching people in the congregation and neighborhood his plural marriage beliefs. Defiantly, Arvin announced that he didn't believe in Jesus Christ or the church he had belonged to all of his life. The leaders had no choice but to excommunicate him.

Angrily, Arvin stormed from the meeting and went home to make plans for his own religion.

Ogden Municipal Building
Source: ogdencity.com

STUDENT BODY OFFICERS

took over the job along with the management of student funds, assemblies, dances, sports events, and other functions. They talked their way through daily announcements and student council meetings, attended regional officers meetings, and all kinds of committee meetings, and dug out a toothbrush whenever anyone walked on the Warrior Emblem. They were the "big three", the people's choice, the ones who received top rating on ballots and did the hard work. On their shoulders rested the burden of a successful year. ARVIN, our capable president with his poise, diplomacy, and impressive words, our musical vice-president with her smiling personality, tact, and ability, and our very charming secretary with her helpfulness, and friendliness have successfully shouldered their burdens, turned them into good times and fun for all, and made the school year a really outstanding one.

Arvin, _____ at work in the Library.

Arvin _____ —First place in Oratory at Weber College.

REPÚBLICA DOS ESTADOS UNIDOS DO BRASIL 1ª VIA
FICHA CONSULAR DE QUALIFICAÇÃO
Esta ficha, expedida em duas vias, será entregue à Polícia Marítima e à Imigração no pôrto de destino

Nome por extenso: Arvin George
Admitido em território nacional em caráter: temporário-especial
Nos termos do art. 8 letra o do dec. n. de 1945
Lugar e data de nascimento: EUA, 1 / março de 1930
Nacionalidade: americana Estado civil: solteiro
Filiação (nome do Pai e da Mãe): _____
Profissão: religiosa
Residência no país de origem: Ogden, Utah, EUA.
Observação: permanência em território nacional 3 anos.
FILHOS MENORES DE 18 ANOS

Passaporte n. 354135 expedido pelas autoridades de Depto. Estado em washington na data 11 outubro 1950
visado sob n. 4725
Consulado geral do Brasil em NYork 16 de novembro de 1950

Above:
Source: "U.S. School Yearbooks, 1880-2012"; School Name: Weber High School; Year: 1947

Left:
Visa Source: Ancestry.com. Rio de Janeiro, Brazil, Immigration Cards, 1900-1965 [database on-line]. Lehi, UT, USA: Ancestry.com Operations, Inc., 2016.

DEBATORS
Arvin   (Standing)

L. D. S. SEMINARY

Members of the Weber Seminary have experienced a year packed with activities. A get-acquainted dance was the first social, followed by Thanksgiving and Christmas parties and special programs commemorating all holidays.

Advertising for the senior play, "Family Portrait", was handled by the Seminary as well as the "Know Your Utah" assembly, the purpose of which was to familiarize students with facts concerning Utah.

Church History students were taken on an educational tour of Salt Lake City in April and on May 16, the Graduation exercises and ball were held.

SEMINARY COUNCIL

Arvin

Above:
Source: "U.S. School Yearbooks, 1880-2012"; School Name: Weber High School; Year: 1947

25th Street and the Union Station, Ogden. Photo by Tyler Cahoon, Circa3

3

In Plain Sight

Arvin spent years conjuring up his new religion. In the beginning, he kept most of his ideas secret. Slowly, he began to indoctrinate close family members. In appearance, Arvin was a gentle and harmless-looking man, but he was authoritative and autocratic in his own soft-spoken sort of way. Neighbors and former group members would say Arvin had an unusual control over his wife and children, who seemed to have an unhealthy worship of him and wanted to please him in every way. They believed every word Arvin spoke was true, and they unerringly supported him in whatever belief system he manufactured.

As time went on, Arvin's teachings slowly spread from relative to friend to neighbor to stranger. Many of those who joined his organization had been in previous polygamist groups and were looking for another. Other folks simply thought they were joining a scripture study group. Most recruits were enticed by Arvin's promise that they'd receive more knowledge of God's will than was available to others. What seemed like an innocent activity in self-improvement gradually turned into an association with unusual and perverse expectations and shocking commitments.

Bit by bit, followers came under the spell of Arvin and his deviant teachings. He soon convinced members to sell their homes, which were scattered about Ogden and as far away as California and Montana so they could purchase one within his burgeoning polygamist commune. He called his new "church" the Zion Society, and the god they were required to worship was, in reality, Arvin himself.

It would take several years for Arvin to form his kingdom of perversion in the newly developed Northwood Subdivision in northern Ogden. Unlike most cult leaders who tend to situate their compounds in isolated areas away from prying eyes, Arvin would establish his in plain sight, and neighbors became suspicious.

As folks in the neighborhood began noticing unusual behavior surrounding the new residents, gossip spread quickly, far and wide. The local newspaper got wind of the rumors and assigned reporters to write an exposé about the group. Neighbors were interviewed and they portrayed group members as secretive—saying they shunned outsiders. They described the leader as a charismatic man with "almost a mesmerizing influence over his followers."[1] They said cult members dressed well and were always seen in shirts and ties or dresses and high heels. Reporters noted that the most striking anomaly was the beautifully designed and immaculately manicured gardens surrounding the member's homes, which was not the norm for this neighborhood.

Many neighbors stated the group members were extremists who promoted a doomsday mentality and were preparing for the end of the world. Some claimed the group was planning to take over their neighborhood by purchasing all the homes one by one. Arvin would proclaim, "One day we will have to fight our neighbors," boasting that the cult was "well-armed and will definitely fight."[2]

When reporters confronted Arvin with questions about a polygamist cult, he emphatically denied any such group existed and said he did not believe in polygamy. One of the women in the cult responded to the rumors. "We're just friends. We like each other. That's what binds most people together," she said. And then, with her voice dripping with sarcasm, added, "People think there's something going on out here because our lawns look nice. There's something wrong with that, I guess." [3]

Although cult members denied the many rumors that were circulating, the gossip persisted. As the years went by, suspicions grew, and neighbors went on the look-out for any kind of odd behavior. Folks insisted they tried to be neighborly and would wave to cult members if they saw them in their yards, but their gestures were ignored. They said the children in the group were very quiet and were not allowed to play with other kids in the neighborhood. The children were never seen playing and were only seen outdoors when pulling weeds, picking up leaves, or cultivating gardens. One outraged mother forbade her son from going near the cult's homes after some teenage girls in the group exposed themselves to him as he played outdoors.

There were widespread rumors about a baby or two that died at birth because the group would not seek medical attention. Instead, they handled the deliveries themselves.

Several neighbors witnessed late-night activity between the homes as cult members moved boxes of items from one house to another. Carloads of supplies would arrive at night and would then be distributed between the homes. It was obvious the group did not wish to be seen doing whatever it was they were doing. One neighbor vividly described hearing the nightly click-click sound of high heels moving from house to house after dark.

At one point, one of the men in the cult curiously moved from his home near Arvin to one a block away. The new home just happened to be next door to the bishop of the Latter-day Saint congregation in the area. Arvin had become paranoid and suspected the general leadership of the Latter-day Saint church in Salt Lake City was directing the bishop to spy on the group. Moving to the new house was considered a strategic measure for the cult. Arvin directed the cult member to keep an eye on the bishop while the bishop supposedly kept an eye on the group. The bishop noticed the home of this cult member was never left unattended and reported he and his family were watched constantly.

Neighbors became anxious when they noticed each home had an intricate alarm system installed. The houses had small white lights hidden under the eaves of the rooftops which would be turned on if someone unknown entered the neighborhood. One neighbor worked at a local security business, and the group asked his advice about installing security systems. Enough security equipment was purchased to outfit all the cult's homes with sirens and interconnected warning systems. The company was not allowed to install the systems, however. Men from the cult did all the installations.

The women in the neighborhood were invited to many lingerie parties thrown by the group in an effort to recruit new members. Cult members were also known to come to the aid of women in the neighborhood when needed, such as helping with a flat tire. However, members of the group would never engage with the neighborhood men.

As cult members busily pursued recruits with parties, dinner invitations, and help with home improvements, Arvin did his part by cruising Interstate 15, looking for motorists in distress and hoping to offer assistance.

One day Arvin kicked one of his daughters out of his house. Neighbors noticed he had thrown all her belongings on the front lawn. The 12-year-old girl confided to a youth leader at the local Latter-day Saint church that Arvin was forcing her to marry a man in the group and become one of his polygamist wives. The girl was distraught, and the bishop's family took her in until a foster family could be arranged. This bold young girl narrowly escaped the horrors that were ahead of her and found refuge in a loving family.

One young Latter-day Saint couple living in the neighborhood came perilously close to being seduced by the group.

"They were so nice," the husband said. "We were newly married, and we were both working. Our house had just been built and had no landscaping at the time. One of the cult members lived next door and asked if we would like some help putting in our yard. We, of course, said 'sure.' We came home from work one day to find grass, bushes, and trees beautifully arranged in our yard. We felt bad we hadn't been there to help but when we asked what we could do, he told us, nothing—that he had to do it himself because he prayed about each plant and where God wanted it planted. We thought that was a bit weird, but we accepted his generosity and thanked him."

The couple was invited to dinners and scripture study nights with the neighbor. It all seemed very neighborly to them. One evening the discussion turned to preparedness—storing food and other essential needs in case of an emergency. The couple was trying to build up their own food storage and as soon as the neighbor heard about it, he ran to Arvin and told him they were prime candidates for their group. The next thing they knew, Arvin joined these evening scripture studies and began teaching his doctrine to them.

Arvin began his lectures by telling the couple a convoluted story about why he had been excommunicated from the Latter-day Saint church. He said his refusal to discontinue teaching his doctrine called the "Guidance of the Holy Spirit," in which he received revelation from God regarding spiritual things, led to his membership being removed. He then went on to tell them that the excommunication was an agreement between him and God that allowed him to reach many more people and teach his beliefs to them. The couple said the explanation somehow made "good sense" to them. They described Arvin's manipulation, "He could teach a thousand truths and sneak in one big lie without you even realizing it."

Over time, the young couple became very close to the group. The members of the cult donated time and money to finish their basement and even stocked it with three years of stored food. The only agreement was that the couple would share their storage items with the rest of the group "when times get hard."

The more obligated the couple felt for the favors they were receiving, the more concerned they became about getting too involved with group. Worry caused the young wife to end up in the hospital emergency room in agony one night with painful, bleeding ulcers. While hospitalized, she received a visit from a few of the cult women who began stealing medicines and supplies while the hospital staff wasn't looking. The young wife was flabbergasted at their explanation, "You're sick because God wants us to take these items." Feeling unwell and confused, she tried to pretend the episode never happened.

A few months later, Arvin and three women from the cult came to the young couple's home. Arvin told the wife that she was one of seven women chosen in the pre-earth life who presented a plan regarding an exclusive organization he called Sister Councils. He quoted Isaiah 4:1-2, "And in that day seven women shall take hold of one man, saying we will eat our own bread, and wear our own apparel: only let us be called by thy name, to take away our reproach. In that day shall the branch of the Lord be beautiful and glorious, and the fruit of the earth shall be excellent and comely for them that are escaped of Israel." Arvin explained that each man in the group was given a Sister Council consisting of several wives.

One of the women from the cult told the wife that she had had many conversations with ancient prophets from the scriptures about Sister Councils. She astonishingly maintained that a prophet rode in her car with her one night, even driving the vehicle for a while.

As the couple quietly listened, it became apparent to Arvin that they were not fully invested in pursuing membership in the group. Arvin then pulled out the big guns and told the young wife that her deceased mother had appeared to him.

"Your mother wants me to tell you how happy and excited she is that her daughter is accepting the doctrine of Sister Councils," he said.

With that, Arvin shocked the couple by explaining his abhorrent training program called the Sexual Way of Life in which the women were taught deviant sexual practices. He used pictures of soft-core and then hard-core pornography to teach the principles. He confided in the husband that he had personally spent more than $40,000 in pornographic material when he authored his instructional manuals.

The young husband was told that he would be given the opportunity to have his own Sister Council. Arvin gave him instructions in the various strategies he could use to help him identify recruits to build his council. The first principle Arvin explained was called Finding the Thread. He explained that each man who had been given a Sister

Council would have a common thread identifying the women he would choose to recruit. Arvin's common thread was women's intimates. He would take one of his wives into a department store and watch women look through lingerie. When he targeted a woman looking at skimpy items, he would send the wife over to strike up a friendship. If all went as planned, the unsuspecting woman would be invited to dinner and given some cult propaganda. Another male cult member had a Sister Council that used the common thread of high heels. Women who wore very high heels were his targets. The young husband was also told the group had success recruiting women who were in vulnerable circumstances. Single and divorced women working in low-income jobs were targeted as well as strippers and exotic dancers.

The more the couple listened to Arvin, the more bizarre and depraved his teachings became. With growing alarm, they decided they had heard enough. They put their home up for sale in order to remove themselves from the cult's influence. Not surprisingly, the cult purchased the couple's home, paying a price well above its listed value.

Once removed from the cult's influence, the young couple realized they had been deceived by a con man. They subsequently referred to Arvin as "a wolf in sheep's clothing."

The residents of Northwood endured years of odd behavior from the cult. However, no evidence ever came forth that any children were being harmed. Many of the neighbors tried to sell their homes and move away from the group. Unfortunately, gossip about the cult had spread so widely, it was nearly impossible. Cult members told residents they would one day own the entire neighborhood.[4]

4

Gardens of Evil

After my initial interview with Erin, I decided to take a drive around the Northwood subdivision which was about four miles north of the municipal building. It was just past dawn and I had eight hours before my next meeting with her. I had driven the modest neighborhood where the so-called Zion Society was located many times before. This time it was more than just curiosity that brought me here. This morning, I was coming with extensive and, quite frankly, unbelievable information about each home Erin claimed was owned by cult members. The details she had provided were astounding. She had even drawn a map of the neighborhood marking which homes belonged to the group. I thought seeing the described houses first-hand would help lend credibility to Erin's shocking allegations.

The arrangement of Ogden's streets in a grid formation of north/ south and east/west streets makes navigating the city relatively easy. While the east and west streets are numbered, the north and south streets are named after U.S. presidents in order of their presidencies. Children growing up in the city have little trouble learning the presidents' names. One block east of Washington Boulevard, Ogden's main street, is Adams Avenue, then Jefferson Avenue, and so on until the city limits end with Buchanan Avenue at the foot of the mountain range. Two streets to the west of Washington Boulevard are named after Lincoln and Grant, skipping Johnson. No one is quite certain why, but speculation is the president was never voted in and he was impeached.

Before driving to the neighborhood, I had researched county records regarding the ownership of the homes. The records seemed to substantiate Erin's knowledge of residents identified as cult members and the houses they owned.

. . .

I pulled into the neighborhood in my old Ford pickup that happened to be filled with yard clippings. I hoped this would help me blend into the neighborhood without attracting too much attention. I stopped to take in the streets of the subdivision that were lined with relatively new and modest houses. I noticed all the homes were similarly built of brick and aluminum siding. Most of the yards were simple with greenish lawns and a bush or two. It was easy to pick out the homes belonging to the cult. The yards of these homes were landscaped elaborately, seeming out of place among the other houses. The Zion Society's yards had beautifully trimmed shrubs, colorful flower gardens, and uniformly shaped trees. Quaint foot bridges and stepping-stones graced meticulously manicured lawns that resembled bright green carpets. There was not a weed or stray leaf to be seen. Not a blade of grass was out of place.

I quickly identified the homes Erin said served as sentries for the group. They sat at the entrance to Adams Avenue, with one on each corner of the intersection. As my truck slowly approached, I had the ominous feeling I was being watched. *Is it just my imagination? Am I being paranoid?* Erin had warned me about the interconnected security system in the homes. My attention was drawn to the windows. Most of the curtains were pulled shut, but a couple of them remained slightly parted. There was no sign of movement outside the homes, and I found myself imagining phones and alarms ringing, alerting cult members of a potential intruder, namely me.

According to Erin, the first home served as the security headquarters and belonged to the group's security expert. This man was supposedly paramilitary trained, a weapon's expert, and a martial artist. He was the sect's firearms and personal protection instructor and his home served as the heartbeat of the cult's security system. He provided early warning whenever a suspicious vehicle or individual entered the community. I could see no movement in or around the home as I drove past it. Perhaps it was too early in the morning—a bit of information that would come in handy later on.

Kitty-corner across the intersection on the northeast corner stood the home indicated as the medical facility for the group. It also served as a security backup. Erin said this home had a stockpile of medical supplies including medicines, both prescription and over the counter.

As I turned south onto Adams Avenue, I drove past the home Erin identified as belonging to a woman named Carla. Erin said she was considered the "right hand" of Arvin. Apparently, this home also served as a sewing facility and housed several sewing machines. Erin explained the group had a lingerie business called "Sweet Things" that operated out of this home. In an effort to create additional income, cult members constructed and sold erotic lingerie to local strippers and other interested people. She said the group would invite potential customers as well as new recruits to special evening modeling shows.

Erin had identified the home to the south of Carla's as the central dormitory for adult women. This home supposedly housed the Sister Council or Arvin's adult "spiritual wives." She said Arvin lived in the house and he and Carla also shared a room there.

Directly across the street to the east of Carla's home was the home belonging to a family in the cult. It was called the Home of Inspiration. Erin said it had originally been a storage unit for weapons but now served as the home to entertain prospective recruits. Shrubbery obscured the home's barred windows from the street.

Looking next door, I saw the home Erin identified as the children's dormitory. She said the young girls who were chosen to be Arvin's "sister wives" lived here to be isolated from their parents. The girls were supervised by several older women who served as headmistresses and were only allowed to see their parents a few times during the year. Erin disclosed there were no telephones in this home. She said the girls who lived here ranged in ages from six to 18. Incredibly, Arvin had approximately 30 "spiritual wives" ranging in age from four to 65.

Erin told me to look for a particular home in the commune that had a large bunker built in the backyard. This was very intriguing, and I drove past this home several times trying to get a good look at it. I had to struggle to see the structure through trees and bushes and could determine only that it was large and elaborately built of rock and railroad ties. Cascading plants hung from terraced gardens built into the walls and roof. It actually took up most of the backyard. Unfortunately, Erin was never told what was in it or its purpose.

While analyzing the location of cult-member's homes, I determined there was a strategic plan for buying up properties in the area, beginning at the Northwood subdivision entrance corner. Closer examination helped me to understand the thought process of Arvin and the leaders of the group. They carefully selected two homes to monitor any vehicle or person who entered into the community from each direction. One home faced north with windows providing views in the northerly and eastern direction. The other home afforded views of everything to the south and west. This configuration was impressive from a counter-surveillance point of view.

The homes of the young girls and the self-proclaimed prophet were carefully nestled in the middle of the commune, protected from suspicious intruders. And finally, the Latter-day Saint bishop's home was neutralized by carefully placing one of Arvin's most trusted associates next door. A general with combat experience couldn't have planned better fortification.

As I drove away from this seemingly peaceful neighborhood adorned with beautiful gardens, I couldn't help but draw a stark contrast to the evil that was allegedly happening behind the sparkling windows and brightly painted doors. I was left with many questions. I wondered why the leader did not try to blend the cult's homes into the neighborhood. Why did he call such attention to them and, ultimately, the cult? Did he think the beautiful surroundings were a disguise to the abominations that were happening inside? Was the beauty that surrounded the homes used as a strategy to convince new recruits the society represented an idealistic lifestyle? Or was landscaping so ingrained in Arvin that the attention he received from his skills overshadowed any conscious game plan?

. . .

When I returned to my office later that morning, I immediately began making a list of experienced officers I could request to help with the investigation. At the top of my list was Dave Lucas, a skilled investigator with whom I had worked a number of violent crimes. Dave was my field training officer when I first joined the Ogden City Police Department. We worked side-by-side for several months, where I observed first-hand his demeanor and his values. Lucas was a laid-back sort of guy. Growing up on the family farm, he learned to work hard and solve problems. He also had the uncanny ability to bond with almost anyone he met. Interrogating criminals came naturally to him. I had watched him closely over the years and always held his interview and investigative style as a model to mirror. Lucas interrogated in a "good ole boy" style. He had the ability to convince the suspect that he was really interested in their description of what happened. He'd say to the suspect, "I'd prefer that you explain to the judge the reasons for the crime, rather than me just telling the facts." His methods were very successful. Since Dave was serving in a leadership position in his church, his religious background could prove helpful. With his name in mind, I called the Ogden City Police Department to speak with Chief Michael Empey, hoping he would allow the detective to help me in the coming weeks.

Chief Empey and I had a long-standing professional and personal relationship that dated back to our days in patrol and SWAT (Special Weapons and Tactics). Even after I left the department and joined the county attorney's office, we continued working undercover STING operations together. On several occasions we would find ourselves holed up together inside an old camper filled with surveillance equipment, watching criminals buying and selling stolen property. We learned a great deal about each other in the process and forged a strong friendship. Although Empey was always a perfect gentleman in conversation, he would turn into a warrior when the chips were down. After hearing my request, he approved Lucas' assistance without hesitation.

OPD 91-13795
8/2/91

CHILDREN'S
DORMITORY

OPD 91-13795
8/2/91

HOME OF INSPIRATION
"SHOWHOUSE"

OPD 91-13795
8/2/91　　　　MEDICAL FACILITY

OPD 91-13795
8/2/91　　　BUNKER,
　　　　　NO SEARCH WARRANT!

Source: Ogden City, Utah Police Department Raid Photo, Technical Services

Map of Zion Society Homes in Northwood Subdivision
Created by Mike King, using ArcGIS by Esri - Imagery by Nearmap

5

Search and Separate

"The Holy Spirit moves upon wives so that they may see more clearly whether their husbands are leading them in the right direction. If they find their husbands to be carnal (worldly) rather than spiritual, they are moved to separate themselves from such men. They are moved to search out the company of others who are led by the Holy Spirit and separate themselves from those who are not. Those who have successfully separated themselves from the world and its influence will be responsible to give all the help and assistance they can to anyone who wants to separate from the world. The group will become a haven of safety and rest to such people and even be responsible to feed, clothe, and shelter them when necessary."

Arvin

When I'd asked Erin to meet with me the day following our initial interview, I'd hoped she wouldn't have time for second thoughts about returning. *Who could blame her if she did?* I asked Detective Lucas to join us for this second interview. Two sets of eyes and ears were always better than one.

When I entered the reception area outside my office, I was relieved to see Erin waiting for me. She seemed to be much more upbeat today. Her eyes seemed brighter as if she had finally gotten a good night's sleep. She brought another woman with her, who she introduced as her aunt Judy. She said Judy had some information to share with me.

For a few minutes, the four of us sat around my desk and chatted about inconsequential things—breaking the ice. Erin asked how I was doing and if the things she told me were troubling. *An understatement.* I told her I was doing well and was anxious to learn more about the Zion Society. With that, our conversation turned serious and the two eagerly began.

. . .

Erin initially became acquainted with four women from the cult when she was working at a beauty and tanning shop owned by Judy. The cult women would come to the shop periodically to get their hair and nails done. They would also gather together in the basement of the shop to use the tanning beds. One of the women, named Carla, was very outspoken and would take charge of the appointments. Over the course of several months, Erin and Judy forged a friendship with the women and soon, the two were being invited to Carla's home in the Northwood Subdivision to have dinner and watch videos. As the women would visit, Erin began sharing personal information. She told how she had grown up in an abusive home and that she was currently struggling in a deteriorating marriage.

One day, Carla invited Erin to come to her home alone, without Judy. Erin had no reason to distrust her new friend, and she accepted her invitation without hesitation. When she arrived, she was introduced to several more women who she was told were neighbors. Erin and the women sat around the living room chatting and getting acquainted. The conversation eventually turned to relationships and the women began asking Erin about her marriage. She was more than happy to confide to the sympathetic women that her marriage was struggling and that she felt trapped in it with no options. She feared she would lose her young daughter if she tried to get out a divorce. Adding to her challenges, Erin had just learned she was pregnant again. Interestingly, all of the women shared how they, too, had come from bad marriages and dire circumstances. They said they felt fortunate to have found each other and to have formed such close-knit friendships. They told her they had created a support system to care for each other that included help with finances, food, and child-care.

"We'd really like to help you, Erin," said Carla. "Because we've come from similar circumstances and know how hard your situation is, we'd like to give you and your daughter a place to live. You are welcome to stay here, free of charge, until you can get back on your feet."

Erin weighed her options and they seemed very limited to her. If she chose to leave her husband and marriage, she would not have enough money to support herself. If she stayed with him, and the relationship didn't improve, she felt the stress could be detrimental to her baby. She had suffered five previous miscarriages that she attributed to the stress in her marriage. Erin had endured abuse throughout her life and eagerly responded to Carla's invitation, as she would have done with anyone who showed her compassion or kindness.

One day, Carla invited Erin to her home to measure her for maternity clothes. She told Erin she wanted to help her out and the clothes were free of charge. Carla then made arrangements for Erin to live in the home. Erin was extremely touched by the kindness and realized if she took advantage of the offer she could get out of her marriage.

Just two days later, Erin moved into what she believed was Carla's home. She took her six-year-old daughter with her without letting her husband know where she was going or her intention to divorce him. Her husband, Mark, learned of their disappearance later that evening. He called Erin's aunt Judy to see if she knew anything. Judy told him she sensed something was seriously wrong with Erin, that she seemed very withdrawn and down. She said she had tried talking to her several times, but all Erin could talk about were her new friends, their beautiful homes and their well-behaved children. Judy couldn't help but feel Erin was not the same person she had always known; she was different.

Judy suggested Mark give Erin a day or two to think, assuming she would call him and offer an explanation.

"Erin is supposed to work at the beauty shop tomorrow. I'll talk to her and see if I can figure out what's going on," she said.

When Erin didn't show up for work the following day, Judy called Carla and asked to speak to her. Carla explained that Erin wasn't around and was probably at a doctor's appointment. Judy hung up and immediately called Erin's doctor. The receptionist confirmed there was no appointment scheduled that day. Frustrated, Judy called Carla back.

"Erin doesn't have a doctor's appointment today. I just spoke with his office."

"Ok, look. Erin asked me to tell you she would not be back to work for at least two weeks while she gets her life together and gets squared around," Carla said sternly. And then her tone changed. "Please don't tell her husband where she is. Erin wants to write him a letter to explain her intentions," she said softly.

Judy hung up the phone and replayed in her mind what she had been told. She couldn't understand why she was being prevented from speaking to Erin and instead had to deal with Carla as an intermediary.

Just then Mark walked into the beauty salon. "Judy, where is Erin?"

"I don't know," Judy responded awkwardly.

Judy was a terrible liar and Mark saw right through it. "I know you know where she is, Judy. Tell me."

"Alright, I do know but I can't tell you," she said, unable to meet his eyes.

"Is she with those women she's been talking about?" he asked.

Judy broke down and admitted she was. Furious now, Mark demanded to know why. It was a question Judy couldn't answer. She told him she thought Erin may have moved in with Carla.

"I'm going to go get her," he said.

Judy had witnessed Mark's rage before and worried he might hurt someone if he lost control. She offered to accompany him in hopes of keeping the situation from getting out of hand as they tried to convince Erin to come home.

Judy decided to take her adult daughter along with them for support. When the three approached the neighborhood, she convinced Mark to park a few blocks away and wait. Judy and her daughter would then walk to the house in hopes of talking to Erin. Mark had agreed begrudgingly, telling Judy she had 20 minutes to get Erin, his daughter, and their belongings, or he would.

When the two women approached Carla's home, an older, soft-spoken man in over-sized glasses and unkempt clothes greeted her at the door.

"We're looking for Erin Anderson. Is she here?" asked Judy.

"No, she isn't," he said.

"Do you expect her back soon?"

The man told her that he expected Erin to return in a short time and invited the two to wait inside. Judy, however, felt uncomfortable with that. She thanked him, saying they would wait on the curb.

The two had waited ten or fifteen minutes in the February chill when the same man came out again and said, "I hate to see you sit out here. It's a little cold."

"Do you know if Erin's daughter is here? We'd like to see her. Can you help?" Judy asked.

The man led the two women across the street and into another home. Judy thought it was strange that this man roamed freely from home to home. Once inside, they were greeted by several women all wearing dresses and high heels.

"This woman would like to see Erin's daughter," he announced and motioned for the visitors to sit down. He then walked out of the house, leaving the women alone. Within a few minutes, Erin's little daughter stepped quietly into the room. She seemed nervous and Judy thought she looked very different. The child, who only weeks earlier had stayed in Judy's home several days a week, inched timidly toward her. Judy reached out her arms, "Come and give Aunt Judy a hug." Apprehensively, the child walked toward Judy while keeping her eyes on the other women who stood watching. Judy had an uneasy feeling as she put her arms around the little girl. The room seemed dark, almost evil, and she began to feel short of breath as though something was crushing her chest. She turned to her daughter and whispered, "We've got to get out of here."

Judy took the child by the hand. "Honey, can I talk to you for a minute? Would you like to go get an ice cream cone?"

One of the women interrupted, "Erin requested that no one take her. We are in charge of the child."

Judy had been worried Mark might drive up and create a scene, but now she hoped he would so she could run the child to his car. She ignored the woman and started walking the little girl toward the door. The woman began screaming, "Go get Arvin! Go get Arvin!"

As Judy frantically opened the door, the soft-spoken older man in glasses she now realized was Arvin stood in the doorway. Cornered, Judy and her daughter tried to push past him with the child. Suddenly, Arvin struck Judy's daughter in the face and shoved Judy against a wall. Judy screamed, "Don't push me and don't hit my daughter again, or I'll have you arrested for assault!"

Arvin shouted for the women in the house to call 9-1-1. As Judy turned to leave again, Arvin pushed her even harder. She spun around and slapped him, knocking the glasses off of his face. A woman came running and pulled the child from Judy's grasp. Then several others pushed Judy and her daughter out the door.

"This is nothing but a cult and a devil worship!" Judy yelled as they slammed the door in her face.

Judy and her daughter ran down the street, stopping at one of the houses not belonging to the cult and asked to use a phone to call 9-1-1. The dispatcher told her that police had already been called, and officers were on their way.

As soon as the police arrived, they took down Arvin's story first. When the officers finally spoke to Judy, she told them she and her daughter had been assaulted. The officers were unsympathetic. Instead, the police informed Judy and her daughter they were lucky they weren't being charged with burglary for entering the home with intent to commit felony kidnapping. As Judy argued with the responding police officers, Erin pulled into the driveway and got out of her car.

"Erin, talk to me," Judy pleaded.

Suddenly, Carla appeared and ran to the car. She grabbed Erin's arm and escorted her quickly past Judy into the house. Mark then drove up to the scene as one of the officers followed Carla and Erin into the house. After a few minutes, the officer came out to report Erin did not want to talk to them, and she didn't want any of them to come back, ever.

"They will have you arrested for trespassing if you return," the officer said.

Mark began arguing with the officer and demanded to see his daughter. He was told it was a civil matter, and he should get an attorney. Defeated, the three drove away with Judy crying and Mark fuming.

Carla used the incident to support her efforts in separating Erin from her family.

"See, you were right to leave him and come here where we can keep you safe. Look how crazy they were acting. They all came to kidnap your daughter, but she is safe with us. Your family has turned on you and now they are supporting your husband."

. . .

Erin stopped her story. "It made sense to me. I was dazed and confused. I was thinking, what just happened? All I wanted to do was leave my husband and now I'd lost my entire family too."

She went on to say that within a week of arriving at Carla's home, an undeniable sense of depression came over her and she wondered if she were being drugged.

"For more than a month I felt like I was in a deep, dark fog. I had difficulty thinking for myself or making even the most basic decisions," she said.

While Erin was so disconnected from reality, her daughter was taken from her and placed in the care of some of the other women in the group.

"I was confused, depressed, and barely able to think for myself, so I willingly let them take her. I don't know how long it took, weeks or even months, but I slowly came out of the fog, and I began joining in the day-to-day activities of the group."

6

Grooming Tactics

"It is therefore essential that a program be established to qualify individuals to function in a Zion Society. It must be a program designed to eliminate the carnal characteristics from one's life, cut off the influence of the adversary, and teach one to live under the directions of the Holy Spirit."

Arvin

The next day, Detective Lucas and I sat down with Erin for our third interview. We had taken down so much information already, we wondered how many more layers there could possibly be to this horrendous story. Erin had been dependable, consistent, and believable throughout. However, I still asked myself if there was more motivation to her confessions than her feelings of guilt and her desire to rescue the children she claimed were being abused.

Erin then proceeded to disclose bizarre details of the Zion Society Cult's philosophies and doctrine.

"Most of the women in the group are considered Arvin's 'spiritual wives,'" she began.

Lucas and I glanced at each other and then back at Erin.

She continued. "As I said before, Arvin believed he was a prophet of God and that he had been assigned by God to organize the religious group of people he named, the Zion Society. All the members believed that Arvin was a prophet; some believed he was a god."

Erin took a deep breath and continued, "The group claimed to have additional light and knowledge of God's will. In their minds, they were special and elect like those of the City of Enoch, so worthy that God himself would soon take them all swiftly to heaven. Arvin would say they had special understanding and knowledge that set them apart from everyone else. He said they were protectors of truth and a strength that others could lean upon. We were expected to invite those of like minds to come and join in their so-called 'great and important work.'"

. . .

In her early days of living in the cult, Erin regarded Arvin as mysterious, having spoken to him only a few times. He had arranged for her to use the group's attorney to begin her divorce proceedings and met with her periodically about the arrangements. Despite the fact he had remained quite distant from her, she found herself gravitating toward him for some reason.

Besides his bold declarations about being a prophet who God spoke to regularly, Erin noticed several quirks about Arvin. He demanded perfection in every aspect of his followers' lives—whether it be in their yards, home interiors, food, weight, clothing, words, actions, or spirituality. And he created endless rules to obtain his view of perfection. But the standards Arvin insisted on in others apparently didn't pertain to him. His daily ill-fitting wardrobe of inexpensive khaki pants and light blue shirts added to his disheveled appearance. Weight must not have been a requirement for Arvin, personally, since his stomach hung over his belt.

Although he professed to be an authority on scripture and expected daily scripture reading from the group members, he never held any kind of worship service. Group meetings were only held to correct cult members' behaviors. Arvin demanded respect and admiration, and no one in the group dared disagree with him. He spoke softly yet authoritatively but had difficulty pronouncing the letter "s." The sound produced a strange whistle that whirred through his teeth. He seemed to love licorice and carried pieces of the candy in his pockets. Tables were topped with small dishes full of black licorice, and he encouraged the women and girls to eat the candy even though most hated the taste.

When Erin had been living in the group for a few months, Carla came to her room and presented pages and pages of Arvin's religious ramblings. Erin was surprised to learn she was expected to read them all. In an attempt to sound religiously legitimate, Arvin had taken elements of the Latter-day Saint faith specifically and Christianity in general and then twisted and perverted them to meet his own needs. To further manipulate his followers, he used language that had a familiar scriptural ring to it.

Reading through the material, Erin learned Arvin not only considered himself to be a prophet of God, but he also claimed to have served in a heavenly pre-earth life as an instructor to everyone who has ever been born on the earth, preparing them for their earth life.

Arvin's writings purported that one-third of the people in heaven had rebelled against God. All male, they were cast to eternal damnation and not allowed by God to come to earth. Arvin declared: "Most of those who fought against God in heaven were immediately sent to hell, leaving more women on the earth than men. In His wisdom, God appointed me [Arvin] to assemble the women on earth, create family units, and usher the women into the next life where they will reign as gods."

Erin was left alone to digest the information and try to understand how it applied to her. A few days later, Carla came to Erin's room. She told her she had been instructed by Arvin to teach the qualifications necessary to become a member of the Zion Society. Carla led her to a quiet bedroom in the house, closed the door, and began repeating a declaration from Arvin.

Fervently, she announced, "The blessings derived from the society are real. It is not an abstract theory or experiment, or some hoped for future possibility. It is reality now! A Zion Society has been established!"

By memory, Carla introduced the three elements the cult used to define Zion. "Element number one," she began. "Zion is a people who are pure in heart and who are totally committed to doing God's will. They have a desire to constantly change their lives to ever higher levels of righteous living and they commune personally with God. Number two: Zion is a place of order, cleanliness, and beauty. Their homes are pleasant, orderly, and clean. Their yards and gardens are well-maintained, beautiful, and productive. And lastly, element number three: Zion is a condition where there is peace, unity, and love."

It all sounded fine and noble, and Erin was quite impressed with the ideals espoused.

Carla then handed Erin several mimeographed papers titled The Qualifications for a Zion Society. She opened a three-ring binder and instructed Erin to follow along as she explained the steps that were necessary to "change oneself."

Carla grew very serious as she explained the first step called *Lift the Condemnation.*

"Erin, we know you have not read all the material you have been given. And you have not shared the doctrines of the Zion Society with those you have come in contact with. In order to qualify for forgiveness in this area, it is necessary that you begin doing so immediately."

Erin said nothing.

Next, Carla told her that she must *Become Born of God.*

"It is necessary that you become 'alive to spiritual things,'" Carla said. "You must forsake anything that isn't in-line with Arvin's teachings. Only then, will you begin to recognize the difference between Zion and Babylon." She instructed Erin to put more emphasis on this particular step. "Because you obviously don't have a clear picture of the differences between Zion and Babylon (which Carla made sure Erin knew were 'code names' used by God when he spoke of good and evil), you will never understand when you are making bad choices. That is why you need to do everything we tell you."

Carla then skimmed over several steps. *Understanding Spiritual, Carnal and Evil, Obtaining the Guidance of the Holy Spirit, Search and Separate Program,* and Attaining the Higher Level were explained in vague and confusing terms. Erin tried to ask questions, but Carla slyly evaded them.

Carla continued, "*Living the Law of Consecration and Stewardship* is a higher law of economics. Let me tell you a story that Arvin uses to help explain his program called Cooperative Economics. Arvin spent several hours making cinnamon rolls for the group one day only to find he had used salt rather than sugar in the dough. He said there was too much of one ingredient and not enough of the other. In other words, too much salt (representing selfishness) and not enough sugar (representing selflessness) created a distasteful rather than delicious food." Erin found this explanation equally ambiguous.

Carla ended these instructions with *Preparing for the Days of Tribulation*, which meant making preparations for the end of the world and, finally, *Establishing a Zion Level Home*, which Erin was told meant keeping a home of order and beauty.

"Now, Erin, you must follow four steps in order to bring about change in yourself," Carla continued. "Those steps are: illustrate, separate, elevate, and conquer. The Lord finds a way to illustrate certain truths to your heart; he has already separated you from your associates and environment. Now you can be elevated to a higher level of understanding and conduct and will be qualified to conquer the work the Lord desires of you if you obey the things Arvin teaches."

And then Carla became more somber. "Remember, Zion is a condition," she said. "We know of no one who ever qualified for Zion without these truths. It is unimportant to us what your educational, business, or religious background is or what personal experiences you've had. If Zion needed what you've got, it would still be waiting to be established. So put this into the proper perspective and understand Zion doesn't need anything you have to make Zion succeed. It is already a success!"

And then in a motherly way, Carla admonished, "Think about what I've just taught you, Erin. Pray about it." She paused a moment and then added, "And now, you must also pray about who your eternal companion should be." She closed her binder and promptly left the room.

Chills ran down Erin's spine. Carla's final statement confirmed her initial fears—she was involved in a polygamist-type cult. Horrified, she realized she was numbered among a group of women who "belonged" to Arvin. She felt completely overwhelmed with all the gibberish she had just been fed and frantically began reassessing her options. She had burned her family ties and couldn't return to her failed marriage, especially after filing for divorce. Her biggest concern was losing custody of her daughter. She reasoned that staying in the group might be the only way to ensure they remain together where she could protect her. Erin felt her six-year-old daughter was well cared for, especially given the fact that she had not been able to provide that care because of the "fog" she had been in. She couldn't understand why this fuzzy feeling had persisted or what had been causing it.

Nonetheless, the place she was now living seemed almost utopian, and her new friends, although peculiar, seemed to care for her. After what seemed like hours of introspection and contemplation, she said to herself, "If all I have to do is act like I believe in all this in order for me and my daughter to be taken care of, all without a financial burden, I can do this." She became determined to play along with the group's peculiar beliefs. She tried to mirror the others' behaviors, assuming it was what Arvin wanted and that it was the best way to get along and be accepted. As the women gained more trust in her, they showed more support and kindness, something Erin had not felt for a long time. She felt they truly loved her.

7
Sister Councils

"Sister Councils cannot be understood by the carnal mind or accepted by the worldly. In mortality, the carnal and evil dominates the lives of almost all men and women. Therefore, the tender and joyous association possible among sisters of a family unit is seldom ever revealed to those in this world. The proper practice of plurality of wives is not fit for the carnal world."

Arvin

As Erin talked, she delved deeper and deeper into Arvin's mentality and his cult's practices. She explained that Arvin had created groups called Sister Councils that consisted of one man and several women and girls. She recounted a disturbing conversation she had one day with Arvin.

. . .

A few days after Carla had taught her lessons on the Zion Society, Arvin came to Erin's room. He said he wanted her to move to an even higher spiritual level than the program Carla had already taught her.

He closed the door, sat down on Erin's bed, and motioned for her to sit next to him. "It is time for you to learn about eternal families," he said. In a grandfatherly way, he continued. "An eternal family is composed of a husband and wife, or wives, and subsequently, the children resulting from their union. Erin, great power is given to the man and his women who come to this oneness, leaving us to only imagine how incomparable the power is in a family unit that has a sister program where the wives experience sexual love, one with another."

Erin's heart began racing as she tried to grasp his meaning. Arvin continued, "It becomes a program without bonds or limitations for all eternity. We cannot be unified with God without living the Spiritual Way of Life and we cannot be unified with our families without living the Sexual Way of Life. The Lord has told me very plainly, 'If you are not growing and developing sexually you are not spiritual. If a sister cannot relate to her other sisters sexually, she is not spiritual even though she is following the spirit in every other area of her life.' God has made it known to me that the purpose of Sister Councils is to strengthen, unify, and bind the women together; to provide a means to expressing their love, loyalty and devotion. This physical expression of love between the wives is a sacred, holy, and exalting thing. It is spiritual—there is nothing carnal, sensual, or evil. This program is beyond the ability of mortal man to conceive, but is what God intends. This is an elite program that leads women to exaltation."

When Arvin paused, Erin stared at him, stupefied.

He then took both her hands in his and boldly proclaimed his godly authority.

"And God has instructed me to be in charge of my wives, including their spirituality and sexuality."

Utterly shocked by his words, Erin tried not to show it. She sat motionless, saying nothing.

Arvin squeezed her hands and then stood and left the room, and Carla entered. As if scripted, she sat down next to Erin and began discussing the things Arvin had just taught. She began massaging Erin's shoulders and asked what she was thinking. Erin measured her few words very carefully but revealed nothing of her true feelings. Within minutes, Carla asked her if she had been praying about who her companion was supposed to be. Caught off guard, Erin knew she had to answer correctly.

"Is it Arvin?" she asked warily.

Exuberantly, Carla exclaimed, "Oh yes, yes, you are listening to the right spirit. You and Arvin are supposed to be spiritual husband and wife."

Erin sat dumbfounded as Carla called out into the hallway for someone to get Arvin.

Within a few minutes, Arvin came back into the room and knelt down next to the two women. He looked directly into Erin's eyes.

"Isn't she pretty?" asked Carla.

"Yes, very beautiful," he replied. "I'm glad you understand that we are supposed to be together."

Almost casually, he reached over and started sexually assaulting Erin while Carla looked on. Erin stiffened, pulled away, and began to cry. Arvin appeared shocked at Erin's response, and without saying a word, he pushed himself up from the floor and walked away.

Carla became enraged and chastised Erin. "You have offended your master, you have offended your god!" she said and stormed out of the room, leaving Erin alone, dazed, and even more confused.

For several days, Erin felt herself ostracized by Arvin and the women. They seemed to go out of their way to avoid her, and when she spoke to them, they responded curtly. She realized it was a form of punishment by the cult. Eventually, she received another visit from Arvin. He walked into her room with an air of authority and told her he came to pray for her. In his prayer he promised that if she diligently prepared herself, she would be "filled with the Spirit" and would complete the special Sister Council training program.

"Erin, you need to know you are now qualified to receive the necessary instruction that will change your life and qualify you for eternal blessings at my side in heaven," he said.

Arvin explained that he received ongoing revelation from God, and acting on that revelation, he created a number of learning aids and manuals that he had authorized Carla to use to teach her about the sister program.

Erin said nothing.

Arvin left the room, and a few of the women from his Sister Council entered and jumped into action. They seemed intent on making Erin see the error of her ways in order to change her attitude and comply to the groups' teachings. They pulled out a felt poster board, a box of prepared words strips, pornographic pictures, and a large, black three-ring binder. The binder contained pages and pages of Arvin's twisted beliefs and revolting teachings he referred to as revelations about Sister Councils.

Resembling a rehearsed performance, the women began teaching that Sister Councils had existed from the beginning of time. They taught that the period of a person's pre-earth life included a time of instruction, led by (none other than of course) Arvin, under God's direct supervision. It was there, in this heavenly classroom, that Arvin would teach God's children that if they remained faithful, they would be given the chance to live in plural marriage families. These families would consist of one worthy man with multiple wives, each who would bear his children and create an unbreakable bond of continued love. In Arvin's "heaven," the man would have relations with all of the wives as often as he'd like. Almost reverently, the women told Erin that Arvin had proclaimed, "God knew these husbands could only satisfy his wives periodically, so he instructed me to teach the wives how to have relations with each other."

Erin's stomach lurched. She felt like a caged animal that couldn't escape its captor. This is all wrong, she thought. She cringed when she realized the true purpose of the group—women were to engage in sex with each other all for the amusement of Arvin.

It was becoming clear to her that Arvin had created his own playhouse of perversion, and the women of his Sister Council were his toys. There was nothing pretend about Arvin's playtime, however. It was disgustingly real.

Erin boldly attempted to challenge the women about Arvin's Sister Councils. Carla was the first to speak in Arvin's defense. "Arvin can do anything he wants with the members of this society. In order to become more spiritual, you must become more sexual and join a Sister Council. You must begin to experience sexual love with your sisters."

Not believing what she heard, Erin shook her head and began to push back harder, but before she could express her opinion, Carla interrupted, repeating rhetoric she learned from Arvin. "There is no substitute, no different way, no better program. The Lord in His wisdom has so decreed. Wise are those sisters who create within their hearts a desire to quickly be about the process to accomplish it."

The other women continued to expose their brainwashing by saying, "This is a 'mark of high distinction' and belongs only to the most faithful who practice this doctrine."

And with broad smiles they added, "Physical associations in the pre-existence accompanied a bond, with an oath between each member of the eternal family unit that they would seek out one another once they came to earth. Erin, God has led us to you so that we can complete our promise made in heaven."

Carla went on with her presentation by telling Erin that few men in heaven were willing to engage in building Sister Councils on earth.

"Arvin was one of those who knew that his happiness and advancement in the eternities was dependent upon his own efforts, as well as the efforts of the women under his command. We must diligently learn, practice, and be faithful to Arvin in order to achieve heavenly exaltation with him. No effort is too great to make it work, no detail too small or insignificant to be learned and practiced. Perfection is the ultimate goal for us individually and as members of Arvin's kingdom," she proclaimed.

And with that, Carla told Erin that it was time she learned the doctrine called The Sexual Way of Life. With dramatic flair, she looked directly into Erin's eyes and said, "The information you will be learning cannot be understood by people with a 'carnal' mind. These things were given to Arvin directly from God. I promise you that if you will allow your mind to be expanded and enlightened, you will come to trust these sacred truths and be found worthy to be one of the sets of hands of those who are subject to inspiration from heavenly forces."

And then, in Academy Award-winning fashion, Carla declared it was time for Erin to be taught the spiritual expression of sister love. On cue, tears welled up in Carla's eyes as she quoted one of Arvin's revelations. "I, God, grant the joy and far-reaching privilege of physical love. Its divine purpose is to strengthen, unify, and bind them together, and to provide a means of expressing their love, loyalty, and devotion, that in their family unit they may obtain a fulness of joy and be one in all things."

Satisfied with the powerful delivery of her message, Carla stopped talking and sat back in her chair. She glared at Erin as if she were waiting for her to jump to her feet and exclaim, "Hallelujah!"

Now that the presentation had ended, Carla's demeanor suddenly became threatening. "The rejection of the principles you have been taught would only signify that you are looking toward Babylon, rather than toward heavenly pursuits." She then warned Erin to never tell anyone about the concept of Sister Councils, plural marriages, or the special permission the women had received to have relationships with each other.

"This sister program must never be revealed to those in the world," Carla said.

She then closed the three-ring binder and cheerfully announced, "That's enough for tonight. Now, let's play a game we call, Rape in the Dark."

8

Indoctrination

"It has been noted that the glory of man is woman. The sister's faithfulness is the man's glory. Their weakness is the shame he bears. The man is required to accept the responsibility for the sisters in his kingdom. Their lack of faithfulness is his pain. Their devotion is his joy. All things have their opposites. If a woman is not the glory of man, then she becomes his shame and degradation."

Arvin

The night Carla included Erin in a repulsive sex game that involved children, Erin used her pregnancy as an excuse for not playing and just watched. The women and the little girls gathered in the basement of the children's dormitory and Carla gleefully instructed everyone to sit in a circle. She then explained that they would play a game that used cards, a game called Rape in the Dark. One of the cards was labeled "rape." The rules of the game were that whoever got the game's "rape" card was required to engage in sexual play with the other girls. When the game began, Erin was so repulsed that she ran to her room. Shaking with emotion, she found it strange that no one had followed her, and the game seemed to continue as if nothing had happened.

Lying on her bed crying, Erin could hear the women in the room below as they laughed and played. She pulled a pillow over her head to dim the sounds, but nothing could erase what she had just seen and heard.

Several hours later, Arvin entered Erin's room with Carla and expressed his concern for her. He told her he was willing to offer a prayer of comfort and support if she would like it.

"I know it will help you come to an understanding of the special nature of sister programs and the role a game like that plays in developing a sense of closeness with your sister-wives," he said. "Please understand this, Erin; no one is interested in your pre-conceived opinions or beliefs." He paused and glared at her.

"We are not about to adapt ourselves or our beliefs to you, and you are wasting our time when you express them. It's a waste of my time. It is time for you to leave Babylon and join us. If, in the process of being taught, you encounter truths that harmonize with those you already believe, then consider yourself blessed. You are not alone. No one has come to us that didn't need to be taught the correct way, so listen, learn, and then quickly change."

Arvin then sat down on the bed next to Erin and again began to make sexual advances toward her as, once again, Carla watched. This time Erin was careful in her reaction. Instead of pulling back, she spoke politely and again used her pregnancy as an excuse not to participate. Nonetheless, Carla pressured her to give in to Arvin, now with a more understanding disposition. She reminded her that she was now a spiritual wife of Arvin's, something she should be very proud of.

"A sister program provides you with a haven of peace, love, and opportunity for eternal advancement, where you will establish a kingdom with Arvin and all of us. No sister advances alone without Arvin. No sister advances to the higher realms unless she belongs to his kingdom. This kingdom consists of Arvin and his wives who serve him," said Carla

With that, Arvin and Carla seemed to accept Erin's excuse and left the room.

Later in the evening, several of the other women in Arvin's Sister Council entered Erin's room and knelt around her bed. They offered prayers on her behalf and gave her words of encouragement. They told her that through increased faithfulness and prayer, she could be filled with the spirit and become converted to the beliefs of the group, including her new role as one of Arvin's eternal companions.

When they left, Erin sat in the dark, alone, scared, and confused. Her heart sank as she realized she would have to comply or be rejected by the people she now depended upon.

As time went on, however, Erin began to justify Arvin's assault. She eventually convinced herself that living in a polygamist relationship might not be that bad. Erin was completely unaware she was being brainwashed. All that mattered to her was that she was surrounded by a group of people who seemed to love and understand her.

As if Arvin's harem called the Sister Council wasn't disgusting enough, it wouldn't compare to the leader's eventual instructions that would take on a whole new level of deviance. His perverse needs were growing, and like a habit-forming drug, they were becoming more difficult to satisfy. He tried to fulfill his needs by pretending to have ongoing revelations from God about sex. He created a handbook of instructions called The Sexual Way of Life and directed the women in his Sister Council to teach the children from it. The instruction included lessons on seduction, how to set up a sensual environment, and sex acts. The children were taught that to become spiritual they needed to be intimate with Arvin.

Each woman was assigned to teach a different lesson from the manual. They taught the girls they were special and should feel honored to be chosen by Arvin to be his "spiritual" wife. And although they understood they had to have sex with him, the girls were programmed to feel special because they were qualified—they were thin enough, pretty enough, and "spiritual" enough. Most importantly, they were told God was pleased with them and they would be allowed into heaven.

Erin was given the assignment of teaching one of the lessons, and she reluctantly complied. As she did, she felt herself descending again into a deep depression. She recognized the lessons she was teaching were criminal in nature and contributed to sexual assaults being committed on the children by some adults in the group, including Arvin.

Erin was in disbelief of how she had allowed herself to fall into the cult's trap and actually become an accomplice to their criminal acts. The grooming she had fallen victim to had progressed from her being a new and naïve recruit to her being fully involved in illegal acts. In fact, Erin had become trusted enough that Arvin eventually made her his personal secretary.

. . .

Lucas and I glanced at each other periodically as we listened to Erin speak, just to make sure we had heard correctly. We were in disbelief. A phrase commonly used by investigators in cases as unbelievable as this one came to my mind—No one could possibly make up a story like this.

According to Erin, she was considered one of approximately 18 of Arvin's "spiritual wives." She was able to name and give the approximate age of each as she counted. Nine were over the age of 20; five were between the age of 12 and 19, and incredibly, four were under the age of 12.

It became obvious to us that Arvin never had any intention of starting his own religion but was using religion to cloak his sexual perversions. Religion was the impetus that initially enticed others into joining the cult. Once followers were completely invested in the group, Arvin subtly and masterfully convinced them to engage in activities that would have repulsed them earlier.

The disturbing story Erin had just told made us realize the followers were under the control of more than one leader. It was obvious Carla held enormous power in this disgusting cult and it was evident she was as sick as Arvin. We needed to know more about her.

9

Alpha Dog

Born in the 1950s, Carla was raised in an average middle-class home in northern Utah with both parents and several siblings. She was well adjusted and happy throughout most of her childhood. As she grew older however, she began to feel as if she couldn't measure up to her parents' expectations, especially those of her father who some described as being controlling and autocratic. He was a devoutly religious man who had served in a number of leadership positions in their local church.

Growing up, Carla continually sought her father's approval. She attended church regularly and as she entered her teen years, she began to develop an obsession with becoming more "spiritual." She read scriptures and prayed excessively. From time to time, she would become critical of the behavior of her friends and would call on them to repent. When they ignored her, she would report them to church leaders.

When Carla was in high school, her parents began questioning some of her decisions. She started dating a boy they did not approve of. Jeff was slightly older, was out of school, and was not interested in church. In their conservative eyes, his "muscle car" and motorcycle hobbies were very concerning. The young couple began spending more and more time together, and as their attraction to each other intensified, Carla's parents became determined to pull them apart.

Consequently, Jeff and Carla eloped before her 18th birthday. Her parents decided that it was best to warmly accept the young man into their family after the marriage, rather than risk losing contact with their daughter. A year later, the couple celebrated the birth of their first child.

Eventually, the couple moved to a small town away from Carla's parents. Here, they both began attending their local church, even accepting church assignments, all while growing their family. They were content with their life until the day a reclusive young couple moved into the neighborhood. In an effort to be neighborly, Carla reached out to the couple and quickly bonded with them. Jeff didn't feel the connection.

While Carla's friendship with the young couple grew, her other friends began to notice significant changes in their relationship with her. Carla became critical and judgmental of her old friends and some of the neighbors. She reverted back to her old ways and began reporting members of their local congregation to church leaders, convinced they were sinning or living improperly. Jeff grew more and more concerned about her behavior, which caused him much embarrassment. He found himself frequently apologizing to the church leaders and neighbors for her actions.

It wasn't long before Carla began losing touch with her old friends. Her closest friend, Kate, eventually reached out to her and was shocked at the changes she noticed in Carla's personality and demeanor. To Kate, Carla seemed very tense and serious. She wondered if Carla and Jeff were having marital problems or if Carla was under some kind of stress. As the two visited with each other in Carla's immaculate home, Kate noticed "a weird little religious book" and wondered what her life-long friend was getting herself into. She noticed Carla could not stop talking about the young couple she had befriended, and Kate couldn't help thinking, *This isn't the Carla I've always known.*

While the two visited, Carla said she had some exciting news to tell Kate and began to speak about "pyramid power" and the healing quality of crystals. She said she had seen their miraculous powers in action at the young couple's home. Kate patiently listened and then said she had things she needed to do at home. As she left, she thought to herself, *Carla's lost her mind. She is as weird as her new friends.*

Carla was changing, and those around her were talking about it. Soon, the changes she was experiencing inside her mind began to manifest themselves in her outward appearance. Carla took on a completely new look and began wearing skirts and dresses exclusively. Her husband was concerned, but his questions were only met with anger and frustration as she accused him of not accepting her for who she was. Carla also began talking about an older man the young couple had introduced her to.

Jeff became alarmed. "Who is this man? What do you know about him?" he asked.

"The man's name is Arvin, and he is wonderful," Carla snapped back. She demanded that Jeff not judge Arvin without knowing him. She even asked Jeff to come with her to meet him sometime.

The next day Carla surprised Kate by showing up at her home unexpectedly. Carla asked if they could find a quiet room to talk, and she began telling Kate all about the Zion Society and its leader, Arvin.

"Kate, I've found this amazing group of people who are living the kind of life I have always dreamed about. They are very religious and so loving and kind." She sounded happier than Kate had heard her in a long time. "The group is taught by an extremely spiritual man who has a remarkable knowledge of the scriptures. I would love you to come with me on my next visit and you can see what I mean."

Kate felt sick to her stomach. She believed Carla was being brainwashed into some kind of weird religion. After thinking about the offer, Kate decided she would go and see what was going on. Perhaps then she'd be able to talk some sense into her friend. She hoped by having a better understanding of this group, she would be able to reason with Carla when they returned home.

When the day of the visit arrived, Kate told Carla that she had some unexpected business she needed to take care of in town. She asked for Arvin's address so she could meet Carla there. As soon as Kate drove into the neighborhood, she noticed the stark contrast in landscaping between several of the modest homes. She pulled into the driveway of the address Carla had given her and was greeted by two women as she got out of her car. The first thing Kate noticed was how eerily similar the women's clothes were to those Carla now wore. They were both dressed in high heels with skirts and blouses that appeared to be homemade. She couldn't help but notice the women spoke in a very distinct way. Their tone was very sweet but disingenuous almost reminiscent of "Stepford Wives."

Despite feeling uncomfortable, Kate followed the women into the house. Here she found Carla in the kitchen preparing a lunch for everyone. She thought it was odd that Carla had ingratiated herself with her new friends enough to prepare a meal in their home.

Once lunch was ready, Carla, Kate, and the women sat down at a large table covered with a feminine tablecloth and set with coordinated tableware. They ate lunch and chatted about trivial things. Suddenly, Arvin walked into the room and introduced himself. As he shook Kate's hand, she felt like he was sizing her up in some way. Seeing this older gentleman with all these women made Kate suspect Carla was getting involved in some kind of polygamist group. She thanked everyone for lunch and excused herself saying she needed to get to her appointment. As she left, Kate thought to herself, *These people are sheep who are following the wrong shepherd.*

As Kate drove out of the Northwood subdivision after what she considered must have been a failed recruitment effort, Carla's husband, Jeff, just happened to be driving into the neighborhood. He'd decided to see for himself what this group was all about and meet Arvin in person.

When Jeff pulled into the driveway, Carla excitedly ran out to greet him with several women following behind. He was introduced to everyone and then invited into the home. The women directed him to sit on the sofa in the living room. Within seconds, Arvin proudly walked into the room and introduced himself. He pulled up a chair directly facing Jeff and casually began to introduce him to the cult's beliefs and the dynamics of the neighborhood. Jeff listened, but could hardly believe his ears.

Just then, Arvin's young adult daughter entered the room. She was ordered to sit on the sofa between Carla and Jeff. Jeff thought this was very odd and carefully edged away from the young woman. He respectfully continued to listen as Arvin wound down his prepared message. He then politely thanked everyone, stood up, and unapologetically said he and Carla had to go.

As the couple drove home, Carla boldly said, "If we move into this neighborhood, Arvin will give you his daughter to be your second wife." Enthusiastically, she added, "I've prayed about it, Jeff, and God has told me she is supposed to spiritually marry you."

Jeff was dumbfounded. "Absolutely not!" he said. "And we are not moving." A deafening silence followed and the two didn't speak the rest of the night.

When morning came, Jeff was still angry. He told Carla he was going to southern Utah to ride motorcycles with his friends for a few days. Carla was unusually supportive of his decision to leave and sympathetically wished him luck as he sorted out his emotions.

When Jeff returned three days later, he was horrified to discover that Carla had withdrawn all their money from their joint business account and moved out. Since she regularly helped with the finances of Jeff's construction company, she had deviously put the money from the business into cashier's checks falsely indicating on them they were payments for subcontracting work. She had planned for various members of the group to cash them as if they were the subcontractors. Luckily for Jeff, the checks were not cashed immediately, and he was able to put a stop payment on them. He was furious with his wife's deceit, but what angered him most was that Carla had taken their children.

Carla was now living in the Zion Society and was fully invested in its teachings. She quickly rose through the ranks to become one of Arvin's "spiritual wives." She callously replaced Alice, Arvin's quiet and ineffectual legal wife of nearly 40 years and became the woman in the group with the most power. Alice mildly slipped into the background while still living in the cult and supporting her husband.

Carla was now second in charge and she became the "mouthpiece" for the self-proclaimed leader. As Arvin fabricated his perverted doctrine, Carla was trusted to deliver the so-called divinely inspired instructions to the group members. One of Arvin's requirements was that members pay him a tithe of their earnings to help finance the group. Carla took pride and joy in chastising the members whenever their offerings to Arvin fell short or when their spirituality wasn't at the level Arvin required.

On one occasion, she criticized the women of the group for not paying enough attention to Arvin. She stated that he had received a revelation telling him some of the women in the group were looking at other men who were not members of the Zion Society. Looking at outside men was considered akin to adultery. This prompted Carla to institute a program in which the women could not go outside of the compound unless there were two or three leaving together. In her mind, this would ensure that the women wouldn't do anything worldly or look at men other than Arvin.

At Arvin's direction, Carla required each of the women and girls to weigh themselves daily. Arvin had determined how much each should weigh and the women were pressured to comply. Arvin also decided on the color each girl was to wear. He authorized Carla to enforce this rule and purchase fabric in the chosen colors so the women could sew their own clothes.

It wasn't long before Carla was exercising more and more power in the group. She began to show as much, if not more, sexual deviance than even Arvin. With him, Carla co-authored the Sexual Way of Life instructional manual. She also devoted much of her time to recruiting women in the community to join the cult.

In order to exert more control over the cult members, Arvin and Carla came up with the idea that everyone should get rid of any "earthly" thing. Subsequently, married couples were required to sell all their jewelry, including wedding rings. The proceeds went to the group, and Arvin decided how they were to be spent. Every photograph of the couple or their family was to be burned, thus erasing any record of the temporal family unit. From that point on, the only family units that were considered valid were those Arvin authorized. In his mind, children living with their birth parents equaled a carnal tie that must be severed. He ordered most of the children to live in homes that were not occupied by their birth parents. Children could visit their parents only when authorized by Arvin or Carla, which rarely happened.

The women and children now looked to Carla for instruction in everyday life. She was the trainer, the enforcer, and the watchdog. Although slight and mousey in appearance, Carla was domineering and aggressive in personality. The children were terrified of her. Their nickname for her was the alpha dog. Aside from Arvin, she held the most power in the group.

10

Any Earthly Thing

The more Erin talked, the more Lucas and I began to understand the Zion Society's inner workings and its leaders' strategies. We were learning to recognize the methods the cult used to manipulate and control its members. By separating the followers from friends and family and then eliminating any memories of their past selves, cult leaders stripped members of their own identity. Followers came to rely on their status as members of the cult for their identity. The cult members became convinced they were unable to make decisions on their own and relied on the leaders to direct their daily lives. It became apparent to us that we were dealing with serious mind control. This dehumanizing process would make rescuing children from the cult extremely difficult.

. . .

Little three-year-old Amber had been born in Michigan to a drug-addicted mother. The two eventually made their way to New Mexico, where, one day, her mother dropped Amber off with a man and his wife to be babysat. She never returned for her. The couple eventually adopted the little girl and a few other children, but the father ended up losing his job and the family became destitute. Consequently, they bounced from place to place before eventually joining a polygamous group. The family stayed for a while until the father began disagreeing with the leader. They then left the group and ended up living in their car or in whatever cheap rooms they could rent.

One afternoon Amber found a beautifully wrapped box sitting on the stoop of their rented room. The electricity had been turned off again, so Amber's adoptive mother lit a kerosene lamp to see who the package was for. There was a small note attached to the box that read, *To Amber, From Someone who loves you.* Amber was giddy with excitement. She carefully opened the package that was wrapped in Christmas paper even though it wasn't December. Inside she found a pretty handmade Raggedy-Ann doll with black-yarned hair. Amber was the only child in the family with dark hair and she wondered how anyone could possibly know how self-conscious she felt because of it. She had always wished she looked like the rest of the family. The doll wore a shiny-satin plaid dress with a white apron and white bloomers underneath. On the body of the doll was a hand-sewn red heart. Amber looked all over the wrapping paper and all through the box to see who sent it but found no clue.

She asked her adoptive mother, "Do you think my real mom left her for me?"

"No. And I'm your real mom."

"I mean my biological mom."

"No, your biological mom was a drug addict."

"I know, but the note said they love me, who could it be?"

"I don't know."

Amber was smiling, laughing, and crying all at once with happiness. Someone loved her enough to do this for her. She had no idea who gave her the gift, but it was at just the right time. She had always felt lost and uncomfortable in her own skin. The doll filled an empty space inside her. For once in her life, she felt special. She named the doll Kristeen Ann and held it close every night.

Amber's adoptive parents continued their vagabond lifestyle until they eventually found the Zion Society. A few days after joining the group, the family was informed they would need to get rid of all their possessions because they represented a carnal tie to worldliness. It was Carla who came to Amber's room and broke her heart. When she saw the beloved doll, Carla immediately took it and told her she would put it away for safe keeping. The doll was never seen again.

. . .

Andrea's parents had been looking for like-minded religious extremists who practiced polygamy when they found the Zion Society. Andrea was twelve years old when her family was introduced to the cult. The parents were overjoyed, believing that they had finally found the ideal community when they moved into one of the split-level homes surrounded by beautiful gardens in the Northwood Subdivision. Andrea immediately began attending a type of home school in a local church with several other students from the community. Like any other pre-teen girl, clothes, makeup, and hair became very important to her, and she was even developing a crush on a boy. To fit in, Andrea purchased her first pair of tapered 501 skinny jeans at a garage sale. She even altered them to fit her better. Having spent her young life in various polygamous fundamentalist groups, Andrea had never been allowed to wear modern clothes. She was finally feeling a part of the outside world, and it boosted her confidence.

Unfortunately for Andrea, it wasn't long before Arvin exerted his enormous influence and convinced her to quit attending the school. He also separated her from her parents and moved her into the Sister Council house as one of his "spiritual wives." Not understanding what it all meant, Andrea felt proud to have been chosen. She was excited when a few of Arvin's other "spiritual wives" took her to a local mall to get all dolled up. Her ears were pierced, and she was given a haircut and perm.

When Andrea's mother found out, she was not happy. She believed God disapproved of pierced ears and she held a strange belief that bangs covered the "third eye," restricting God's access into her soul. Now, however, Andrea's mother had no say in her daughter's upbringing— her daughter belonged to Arvin. Because of all these changes, Andrea was elated with how grown up she felt. She had no idea what lay ahead of her as one of Arvin's "spiritual wives."

One day, one of Arvin's young wives came to help Andrea pack her things for the move into the Sister Council house. Andrea proudly showed off a Norman Rockwell print collection she had been acquiring for quite some time. She had plans to frame each one.

"Oh, you won't be needing those where you're going," said the young woman. "Personal belongings are part of the 'carnal' world and will no longer be a part of your life."

Losing her prized collection was devastating.

Andrea's much-loved jeans were taken as well. Soon, all connections to her past and family were gone. She was no longer considered her parents' child, and every trace of the first twelve years of her life was gone.

PART TWO

"This is no Parade."
    Ogden Police Officer

11

Building the Case

It was just after seven o'clock Monday morning when I sat down at my office desk with my Diet Coke and a day-old doughnut. Lucas walked in shortly after, sat down, and sighed, "Here we go again." Our final interview with Erin would begin soon, and I was hoping the caffeine would kick in because I hadn't slept well since her first visit. The stories of sustained abuse would shock me during the day and haunt me at night, making sleep nearly impossible.

Lucas and I began doing some mental math. If Erin's allegations were true, then 32 children were in constant danger of being sexually abused by the 70 adults who lived in the cult. These were the very people the children trusted and relied on to care for them. Erin had told us that there was daily ongoing sexual instruction and abuse. If true, that meant each child was potentially enduring five or more assaults each week. We were horrified at the magnitude of the abuse.

Erin arrived promptly at 8:30 am and without discussion, we settled into our usual chairs, and I reached for the recorder. On cue, as though rehearsed, Erin nodded, acknowledging that it was time to begin. She displayed confidence throughout, and I reminded myself that only a year and a half earlier she'd been a broken and vulnerable young woman. It was chilling to think how Arvin and Carla had skillfully and methodically brainwashed this young woman, and so many others, to the point that she was willing to break the law to remain in good graces with the self-proclaimed prophet. In fact, doing anything Arvin commanded.

Many of the crimes Erin described seemed unbelievable, and I found myself wondering if she was fabricating the allegations, or at least exaggerating the facts. It seemed every time I thought to myself, *I've heard it all,* she would reveal another scenario that would shock me even more and leave me, once again, questioning her testimony. Today would be no exception.

Erin told us as time went by, she became a trusted friend and mentor to the girls in the cult. One day a few of them came to her with a shocking story they needed to share. They confided in her that Carla had begun selling sex-weekends with the young girls to a man who lived in Logan, a community that was about 50 miles north of Ogden. Carla would make the arrangements and then drive the girls to the man's home to meet up with him. Here they would engage in whatever sexual activities Carla had arranged to receive payment for. On multiple occasions, Carla either watched the assaults or joined in.

I asked Erin to identify who had been abused in those encounters. She was able to give the names and ages of each child. As she spoke, I realized that two of the names were children who had recently been removed from the group as part of a custody battle with an ex-husband.

I know who these children are.

"I'll be right back," I said, and I rushed out of the room to the county attorney's office.

"You're never going to believe what Erin just told me," I said, and then recounted Erin's story to Richards.

"Aren't these the kids of the father you spoke with a few months ago?" I asked.

He thought for a few seconds and then opened the top drawer of his filing cabinet. He began rifling through a stack of yellow legal-size notepads.

"Here it is," he said as he flipped through the pages for something he had written down.

"Yes, here it is! The man's name is Jeff Peterson, and he and his new wife, Kate, asked for help in a custody battle. I've written here that his former wife still lived in the group and didn't allow him to see his children."

Richards explained the couple had expressed concerns that Jeff's children were being subjected to an unacceptable atmosphere that included strange sexual practices among the adults living in the group. He feared that his children were being indoctrinated with plural marriage ideology.

"Since they didn't have any evidence to support their claims, other than 'gut feelings,' I suggested they work with a civil attorney and maybe hire a private investigator," he said.

I returned to my interview with Erin and questioned her specifically about the assaults in Logan. She told me she was very close with the girls and there was always a lot of talk in the group, specifically as it had to do with sexual things.

"Arvin had instructed us all to be bold and daring, but not dangerous," she said.

"I don't understand," I said.

"Arvin directed the women and girls to be sensual and 'show off.' We were expected to tell enticing stories but were warned there was a fine line between being bold and daring and being careful not to expose the group's secret beliefs and practices."

Erin went on to say she was shocked when Jeff's daughter told her she had been assaulted several times by the man in Logan and by Carla, her own mother. These included a number of times when other young girls from the cult were involved in group assaults.

When I asked if any boys were involved, she said she had heard a boy was dropped off with the man for a weekend once but couldn't remember the specifics. She was also aware the boy had been assaulted a number of times by Arvin and some of the other adult members of the group.

Following the interview, I presented Richards with more than enough serious allegations to draft an affidavit petitioning a judge to sign a subpoena that would make it possible for Jeff and Kate to speak with me openly about their custody battle and the stipulations that were placed on them to remain quiet when it was settled.

Two hours later, I was standing in front of Second District Court Judge Stanton M. Taylor, a seasoned adjudicator with a kind yet firm demeanor. I raised my hand and swore that I'd been informed of several incidents of child sexual abuse from a reliable informant who had personal knowledge of the offense. I told him I needed to interview Jeff and Kate Peterson in order to complete the investigation. The judge granted my petition and said, "Good luck, detective."

With the subpoena in hand, I reached for my Motorola "brick" mobile phone and called the Petersons. We set up a time for them to meet me the next day.

The rest of my day passed quickly as I prepared the questions for my interview with the Petersons. I was surprised to see that it was almost 9:30 pm and the sun was just setting. The building was becoming dark. The marble walls that echoed every footstep and conversation during the day were uncomfortably silent.

As I stepped out of the elevator to the main floor, I was startled by the building's security officer. Hoss, as he was affectionately known, had a massive 6'5" frame that was magnified by his tall Stetson cowboy hat.

"Working late, I see," he muttered.

"I lost track of time," I said.

Needing a moment to vent, I shared with him that I was working a serious child sex assault case.

Hoss could sense my stress and placed one of his enormous hands on my shoulders, looked me in the eye, and said, "I hope you get the (expletive), Mike. I hope you get him."

I left the building thinking, *So do I.*

12

Private Investigator

Through searching data bases, I found contact information for Jeff Peterson. I called him the next day and introduced myself. I told him I wanted to talk to him about his ex-wife, Carla, and his children, who were living in the Northwood Subdivision. He seemed quiet and apprehensive at first, but after hearing the purpose of my call, his demeanor quickly changed. He agreed to come to my office the following morning.

"I'll move some things around and be there. Just name the time," he said.

After hanging up, I researched as much as I could about Jeff. I learned he had made several complaints for custodial interference and child custody to no avail.

The following morning, Jeff and his new wife, Kate, sat down for a formal interview with me. Ironically, Kate was Carla's old friend who the cult had tried to recruit several years earlier. Jeff and Kate both went through divorces and later became reacquainted. Kate was aware of Jeff's challenging situation and the custody battles he had been through, and the two bonded over their anger with the cult.

After some initial chit-chat, I opened the credenza and pulled out the court order I had obtained the day before. I slid it across the desk directly in front of Jeff and said, "Please take a moment to review this court order. It releases you from the obligation you entered into in your divorce stipulation. This order makes it possible for you to talk to me about your custody fight with your ex-wife as well as anything you'd like to say about Arvin, the man she is living with."

He looked down at the document and smiled as I outlined all the items the court had agreed he could give me. Books, papers, documents, recordings, or anything else he or Kate felt might be relevant were all approved. I reminded both of them that they needed to keep our conversations confidential. I cautioned them that releasing any of the information we talked about could be harmful to the investigation and, perhaps, the children. And with that formality out of the way, we began our discussion.

I started off by asking Jeff what he could tell me about the group his ex-wife Carla was involved in. He told me that two of his children, a boy and a girl, were being brainwashed with a bizarre doctrine that included separation from their mother and polygamist teachings. His son was five years old at the time and had been born shortly after his ex-wife left him to join the group. Because of that, Jeff had never had a chance to develop a good relationship with the boy. His relationship with his teenage daughter was better, but rarely did either want to visit him.

Jeff then began to tell an extraordinary account of when he had hired a private investigator from Orem, Utah, to find out about the secretive group. He hoped to get enough information to build a case that would warrant him to at least get joint if not full custody of his children.

. . .

After reaching his rope's end in dealing with Carla, Jeff contacted private investigator Phil Naugle, an experienced investigator who owned his own investigation company with his wife, Cheryl. Jeff provided the investigator with all the information he had about his children's situation. As Naugle studied the case he immediately recognized the challenges of getting information about the Zion Society through publicly available sources. Naugle carefully went through Jeff's overall description of the group and zeroed in on a few peculiarities: polygamy, the obsession Arvin had with landscaping, and the lingerie business the group had established.

"That's it," he said, circling the words "Sweet Things" on his note pad. "That's my ticket in."

Naugle called Jeff to ask more questions about the business. Jeff didn't know much, but he told Naugle he did remember a time when Carla asked him if he still had friends in Las Vegas. He recalled that she wanted to know if any of his friends had contacts in the casinos. Carla told him that she thought strippers and dancers might be interested in the lingerie she was making. She even offered him a finder's fee if he could help her locate some buyers for the clothing. It was a comment made in passing and Jeff didn't think about it again until Naugle brought it up.

"Jeff, do you think you could call Carla and tell her you mentioned her lingerie business to one of your friends? Tell her your friend said he might have a buyer who would be interested?"

Jeff caught on to the investigator's plan and said he would call her the following day.

When Naugle hung up the phone he realized his wife, Cheryl, had been standing behind him, eavesdropping on the call.

"What was that all about?" she asked in her natural Southern drawl.

Naugle explained the situation to his stay-at-home wife and said, "If it works, I'm going to have to find a woman to act like a buyer and go in there."

"I'll do it," Cheryl said. "I don't have anything else to do and it would be kind of fun,"

Cheryl was the kind of person who loved being around people. She had an engaging personality and could create a conversation with anyone. She was attractive, petite, and very friendly.

"It's out of the question, Cheryl," Naugle said. "You don't have any investigative training. What would you do if something went wrong? I just don't feel good about it."

"You know me. You know I can talk myself in or out of any situation," she said.

"It's true, you certainly can do that," said Naugle.

Before long, they were crafting a plan.

The next day Jeff called Carla and told her he had run into an old friend in Vegas who happened to have a contact in the casino business. He told her he would have his friend call her, but he couldn't guarantee anything. Carla was ecstatic and thanked him for helping. After hanging up the phone, Jeff updated the private investigator and gave him Carla's phone number. Naugle and Cheryl spent the rest of the day piecing together their plan. Cheryl made her first call to Carla later that week.

When Carla answered the phone, Cheryl introduced herself as a buyer from a casino in Las Vegas. She told Carla she had been given her name by one of her managers.

"My boss told me you have a line of exotic clothing for dancers," she said.

Carla took the bait, hook, line, and sinker as Cheryl delivered her sales pitch.

"I'll be in Salt Lake on Thursday of next week, honey. My flight has a four-hour layover. If you are available, I'll adjust my flight to leave the following morning. I can rent a car at the airport and drive up to meet ya'll," she said.

Carla readily agreed.

Cheryl excitedly reported the details of her conversation to Naugle. Although he was still a little unsure of the idea, he picked up the phone and called Delta Airlines, booking a round trip ticket from McCarran International Airport to Salt Lake International Airport. The plan was to purchase an airplane ticket for a flight that originated in Las Vegas with the correct date to support their cover. Cheryl would have the ticket stored inside her notepad. She would open the notepad in front of Carla to write a few things down and the ticket would fall to the floor.

If everything worked as planned, Carla would pick up the ticket and see that it was from Las Vegas, further legitimizing Cheryl's claim.

On Wednesday evening, Cheryl drove from Provo to Las Vegas and spent the night in an airport hotel room. She boarded Delta Flight #DL1097 at 6:40 am the next day and one hour and 18 minutes later, she exited the plane in Salt Lake and headed to the rental car counter. Around four pm, she drove into the Northwood subdivision. Naugle was already in the neighborhood sitting in a car for backup. They briefly looked at each other as she drove by. Cheryl breathed a sigh of relief, thinking, *He could get to me within seconds if something goes wrong.* The rookie under-cover agent then pulled into the driveway of the Sister Council house.

Cheryl didn't notice the women who were waiting on the porch. Instead, she was busy hiding some of her paperwork, just in case someone looked inside her car. Suddenly, someone opened her car door, startling her. She jumped slightly. When she looked up, she found that an older man was standing in the car doorway. He introduced himself as Arvin. Cheryl immediately felt uncomfortable, and although she found him to be a bit "creepy," she tried to flirt with him just a little.

"Oh my, honey. You startled me a bit. What a gentleman you are to come to my car and greet me."

He grinned. "Carla is inside," he said as he motioned toward the front door of the house.

As Cheryl approached the house, several women jumped into action. Cheryl felt as though she was walking into a rehearsed performance. The women wore toothy smiles as if they were expecting to have their photo taken. They welcomed her enthusiastically. Once inside, Cheryl met Carla who introduced her to several of the adult women who would be modeling the clothing. Carla then took her to the basement to tour the cult's sewing facility and pulled various pieces of lingerie from the shelves that lined the walls. Each suggestive article of clothing was designed around a theme such as cowgirl, French maid, and sailor girl. Cheryl pretended to be interested. "Oh my, the dancers would love these new and exciting designs," she said.

Back upstairs, Cheryl couldn't help but notice how immaculate the home was. Carla showed her to an assigned seat in the living room and directed several 20-something-year-old women to scoot into a back room and change into the lingerie. While the young women were changing, two teenage girls entered the room, including Jeff and Carla's 14-year-old daughter. Carla introduced her young daughter and then changed the subject and began explaining the business operations of "Sweet Things" lingerie.

"It seems there are several women in the neighborhood that are involved in the business," said Cheryl.

"They're just women who like to sew, and they help a little with the construction and design of the products. But that's all."

"So, who is this Arvin?" Cheryl asked.

Carla replied nonchalantly, "Arvin is just a nice gentleman from the area who does everyone's landscaping."

While the girls got dressed for the show, two came into the room without a stitch on, saying they were looking for their body suits. Although Cheryl realized there were only women present, she still thought this to be a bit bold. From their casual demeanor, she got the impression this was something they did all the time. Cheryl asked Carla if the girls could model the clothes without the body suits underneath. Carla agreed as long as the camera was turned off.

The models poked their heads around a temporary curtain they had hung in the hallway and nodded they were ready. Sultry music played from a cassette recorder as one by one, each woman shimmied through the curtains and struck poses while dancing provocatively. It was a B-rated performance in Cheryl's opinion, but the models were on cloud nine, basking in the compliments she was giving them.

Some of the girls wore short nighties and would lift them up coquettishly in front of her, exposing themselves. She thought to herself, *These girls are very bold and not at all modest.* At one point, Cheryl asked if the younger girls ever modeled the clothing. Carla then instructed her 14-year-old daughter and three other young girls to go change and model for Cheryl. She proudly told the private investigator that a local stripper taught all the women, including her daughter, how to dance, in exchange for some G-strings and custom sewing. Carla bragged that her daughter caught on quite quickly and was a natural with the movements. Cheryl could hardly contain her excitement, knowing she had the evidence Jeff needed to claim his daughter was being sexualized.

When the production came to an end, Cheryl laid the compliments on thick and promised to return with an offer. Carla was thrilled. She invited Cheryl to drive out to the group's rented storage facility in the Weber Industrial Park to see their inventory. As the two drove to the facility, Carla continued to tout the "Sweet Things" business.

Once there, the two toured the warehouse where mass quantities of exotic outfits were stored.

"How many buyers does your company have?" asked Cheryl.

"Actually, we don't have any yet," said Carla. "But we just registered for a Boutique Show at the Ogden Union Station. We'll be displaying our merchandise to large crowds, and hopefully, we'll make some sales and possibly develop some local contacts."

As the two women drove back to the subdivision, they engaged in casual conversation. Carla began sharing personal information.

"I'm so excited. I am going to be a grandmother," she gushed. "My sixteen-year-old son got a girl pregnant. I don't know if they'll get married. Personally, I don't think I could ever get married again. I am perfectly happy with my life right now."

Cheryl changed the subject.

"Do the young models attend public schools?"

"Oh no," said Carla. "We run a private school called the Midland Academy and there are about 30 children enrolled. They attend light classes in the summer which are held only in the morning, and during winter months, they go to school all day. The kids really enjoy this type of schooling over the public-school system. And our teachers are certified," she explained.

Cheryl sensed Carla trusted her enough for her to ask one more question. "Does your daughter live with you?"

"No. All the young girls live down the street in the home of another woman. We call it the Children's Boarding School. It's a kind of dormitory and the girls love living together."

As the visit was ending, Carla asked, "Would you like to learn more about our business?"

"I would love to," said Cheryl.

The two agreed they would go to the upcoming boutique show together and then spend the evening discussing the enterprise. As Cheryl drove out of the neighborhood, she felt a rush of excitement. She found that she was really liking investigative work.

Weeks later, with an invitation in hand, Cheryl returned to Ogden and joined Carla in the "Sweet Things" booth at the boutique show. The booth attracted little interest from the public, and Carla justified it as "conservatives' fear of intimate clothing." Later that evening, the two returned to the neighborhood for dinner and movie night with several other women. In what felt like a repeat performance, Cheryl was met by Arvin in the driveway as she arrived. This time she felt like he was checking her out to see if he should allow her to meet with more of the women in the group. She apparently passed the test and was allowed to go inside with Carla.

As the investigator "played along" with small talk, the women became physical in their interactions with her. They hugged her and put their arms around her. Then, Carla unnerved Cheryl by saying she "loved" her and invited her to attend an orientation session to learn about the group's beliefs. With no apprehension, she then asked Cheryl to move in with them. Trying to contain her surprise, Cheryl told Carla she was married, and she'd have to talk to her husband to see how he felt about it.

"Can my husband come to the meeting?" Cheryl asked. Carla said that he could attend later, insisting that Cheryl attend the first session alone.

Three months later, Cheryl arrived at the designated home for the scheduled orientation she was told Arvin would be giving. This time she was met by some women she didn't recognize. They invited her in and said Carla was on her way. Just then, Arvin arrived with Carla, carrying wooden easels, various visual aids, and books. Cheryl now realized the nice gentleman who does everyone's landscaping was actually the cult's leader.

This home was also abnormally clean. So clean, it made Cheryl uncomfortable. She thought to herself, *Cleanliness may be next to godliness, but too much cleanliness is next to mental illness.* She noticed the women in the group talked with the same, peculiar, almost a whispering sing-song voice. They held their lips in a certain smile, and Cheryl felt they all moved in the same way, as if they were under some hypnotic trance.

As Arvin and Carla began teaching their philosophy and doctrine, Cheryl interrupted, "Would you mind if I record your presentation? I'm sure my husband would love to see it."

"That's fine. I have nothing to hide," said Arvin.

The women's strange demeanor suddenly made sense to Cheryl as she listened to Arvin speak. As he began teaching her, he used a soft, smooth tone and she felt he was trying to portray himself as a clergyman of some kind. He never raised his voice but delivered his message in a low, monotone manner. Cheryl felt he chose his very words very carefully. When she asked him pointed questions, he would either dismiss them with a chuckle or ignore them and change the subject.

While trying to be attentive to Arvin's presentation, Cheryl couldn't help but notice the unusual behavior of the children in the home. They were made to sit on the sofa and were not allowed to move or speak unless given permission. They reminded her of little robots, dressed alike, and conducting themselves similarly.

As the presentation was winding down, Arvin asked Cheryl to read some passages out of a book they had given her. She complied, and when she finished, Arvin explained their meaning. She understood neither the passages nor Arvin's explanation of them. Cheryl had patiently sat through several hours of sermons that supported the group's belief that Arvin was a prophet and that God spoke to him. All the while, Cheryl was afraid they'd find out that she wasn't who she said she was. She kept dreading that Arvin would jump up and shout, "You are a phony!"

As the evening came to a close, Cheryl was told she would need to fill out an application in order to be considered for membership into their fold. The application would then be reviewed by Arvin and his Spiritual Committee. She was warned that the members were in-tune with spiritual matters and they could immediately spot a fraud. *Are they seeing through this ruse?* she wondered. Just when she was about to panic, she was told she didn't need to fill out the application after all because they could sense she was "pure in heart" and would be a good fit in the group.

. . .

As he came to the end of the account, Jeff handed me a video and some photographs Cheryl had taken while watching the fashion show. The pictures showed a number of children in sexually explicit clothing posing in provocative ways. Carla's voice could be heard on the video directing the girls' seductive movements.

"That changed everything when we found this out," Jeff said. "I called my ex-wife and told her I wanted the kids immediately or I was going after her and the rest of them with the stuff the investigator had uncovered."

His threat worked. An hour later, he received a call from Carla's attorney, saying, "You can have the kids if you call off the dogs!" He told Peterson to meet with him at his office the next day to make the exchange.

Jeff and Kate seemed to let out a collective sigh of relief as the interview ended. For a moment, I wondered if I should just stop and spare them the anguish of learning the rest of the story. There was a moment of uncomfortable silence.

Kate broke it and asked, "Is there something else you wanted to talk about?"

Looking into their concerned faces, I couldn't help but feel empathy for them.

"I've received some information suggesting that some of your children may have been sexually abused, perhaps multiple times. Were you aware of this, or did you have any suspicions?"

Without flinching, they both nodded their heads. "We've wondered," answered Kate.

Source: Ogden City, Utah Police Department Raid Evidence

13

"No-Knock"

I was told Judge W. Brent West had a full schedule, so I asked the bailiff if he would do me a favor and slip the judge a note asking him to sign a few search warrants. As luck would have it, the two lawyers in the courtroom were discussing a plea negotiation. The judge ordered a court recess and met me in his office.

I had come to know the judge some seven years earlier, during his time as a prosecutor for Ogden City. After he became a judge, our contact became less frequent, but it was always a pleasure bumping into him from time to time. We usually ended our visits with a discussion about football. We were both die-hard Dallas Cowboys fans and loved talking about the glory days of the team. It was one of those silly things that seem to lead to a special friendship. Today however, there was no mention of football.

"Judge West," I said. "I'm in the middle of a complex child sex abuse case and have uncovered enough information to believe the allegations are true. A number of children are living in a cult environment with adults, and I believe the entire group has adopted the leader's philosophy of sex abuse."

The judge listened intently as he studied the paperwork.

"I'm hoping you'll approve this search warrant request so we can serve it as quickly as possible. I'm concerned that with every day that passes, the chances the evidence will be destroyed increases. I also have a petition for the arrest of the cult's leader."

The judge questioned the reasoning behind my request for an early morning raid without notification.

"I believe a "no-knock" warrant is necessary because I fear the defendant will try to flee and his sympathizers might destroy evidence," I explained. "My informant told me the leader had ordered the group months ago to destroy large amounts of pornography because he thought a raid was going to happen. She said they burned boxes and boxes of material. She also told me there were hidden semi-automatic assault rifles in many of the homes as part of their defensive measures, and that many of the residents were proficient with the weapons."

Satisfied, the judge had me hold up my right hand and swear to the truthfulness of the affidavit. I was quite sure we would find enough evidence to arrest Arvin, but I worried he would lawyer-up and not speak to me about the charges. As I walked out of the judge's office with the warrants, I realized that I had placed my personal credibility on the line. Nevertheless, I was confident I was doing the right thing.

The operation would need the planning skills of the most experienced officers in the police department, and two immediately came to mind. Hurrying down five flights of stairs to the municipal building's main floor, I once again headed directly to Chief Empey's office. This time, I needed to request some of his most competent officers and nearly half his force to raid the Zion Society.

I showed Chief Empey the search warrants and provided him with a short update on the case. Before I could request the two officers I had in mind, he interrupted me and picked up the phone.

"Pam, will you please see if Moore and Balls can come to my office?"

Chief Empey read my mind. Moments later the very men I had hoped would oversee this raid walked into the office. Captain Marlin Balls was a seasoned commander. He'd worked nearly every assignment policing had to offer. At that time, he was a captain serving as an assistant police chief, essentially running the police department whenever the chief was unavailable. He was well respected among the staff and he was particularly good at dealing with public relations and the media.

Sergeant Don Moore commanded the city's SWAT team. He was 6'4" and a former Army Green Beret, who had an intense, laser-focused personality. I served as one of his SWAT officers for many years and I trusted him with my life. His insight would prove invaluable.

Within minutes, Moore, Balls, and I were sitting in a conference room as I filled them in on the case. With no time to lose, the three of us began planning and organizing the raid and making assignments. We kept the plans confidential, knowing the success of the operation could otherwise be put in jeopardy. It was decided the raid would begin at six am the next morning.

Our team's goals were simple. The cult's leader was to be arrested on multiple counts of child sexual abuse. The children would need to be placed into protective care where they could be interviewed. And lastly, evidence would be collected and processed.

We had been able to get warrants for eight of the twelve homes in the cult and determined each would require a team of at least four police officers. One officer would serve as the team's leader, with three others assigned to secure the scene and the occupants, and then conduct the search. As a security measure, two patrol officers would be stationed near the four homes for which we weren't able to obtain search warrants. These assignments alone would require 40 officers. Still, many more assignments needed to be filled, and the number of personnel required would grow to almost 70.

Each team assigned to raid the homes would report up to Captain Balls, who would serve as the incident commander. The officers would need to execute their individual warrants at exactly 0600 hours when Captain Balls would signal everyone to move in.

After reviewing the search teams' experience and configuration, Sergeant Moore decided that he would keep his SWAT officers on stand-by a block away. His team consisted of five tactical officers, including Moore himself. They also had two K-9 officers assigned to the team and two paramedics. Together, the officers were capable of handling any kind of armed or violent confrontation. Once the homes were secured, they would provide support, transportation, and back up. Recognizing that the raid would draw a lot of attention, we determined that another six patrol officers would be needed for traffic control to block entry into the subdivision.

Collecting evidence would be an important part of the search warrant. Detective Lucas would serve as the evidence custodian, leading a small team of technicians. They would be responsible for "bagging and tagging" each item discovered. Having been through many of the interviews with Erin, Lucas was keenly aware of the kind of evidence we were searching for. That insight would prove helpful as he provided triage and oversight of the on-site collection effort. We knew we would not be allowed to return to the homes after the initial raid without another warrant, which posed an interesting challenge.

The search of each home would need to be documented extensively with still and video photography. We decided we would use personnel already assigned to work in technical services that morning. Checking the duty roster revealed Detective Gale Bowcutt was working. Bowcutt was a seasoned police officer who had spent the majority of his career working as a K-9 handler. Every cop who ever responded to a violent situation would breathe a sigh of relief if Bowcutt was assigned to back them up. When he retired his dog, he took advantage of an opening that existed in Tech Services and made the move. He was very proficient in his new role and was supported by Detective John Flink, a reliable and meticulous crime scene processor.

The final piece of the puzzle lay in selecting individuals to interview the children taken into protective custody. We all agreed on three women: Katy Larsen, Loura Ashdown, and Jan Hayes. All experienced social workers, these women were well respected in the investigative and mental health community. They also worked in the recently opened Weber/Morgan Children's Justice Center.

Still convinced that we needed to keep the plan confidential until just before conducting the raid, we were faced with the difficulty of convincing the social workers they were needed at four am for a briefing. Early that afternoon, I made the call. All I could say was that we were planning to take a number of children into protective custody the following morning, and we needed their help. Of course, they wanted more information than I could give them, but they ultimately agreed to clear their calendars and maintain their silence. With less than 24 hours of preparation, the women put together a plan to deal with children who had been brainwashed into accepting abuse. They knew the children would be fearful and distrusting of any authority figure outside the group and would deny any wrongdoing. The women talked through techniques they would need to use with the children to calm and reassure them as much as possible.

The SWAT team was activated, and Sergeant Moore spent the remainder of the day and well into the evening scouting the neighborhood, reviewing floorplans I had obtained from Erin, and rehearsing what the method of assault would be, if needed.

As the workday came to a close, the call went out to nearly 70 officers to "be in the police briefing room with duty equipment at 0400 hours." That evening, Sergeant Moore and I prepared operational maps and contingency plans. Knowing that the individual team leaders would be looking for the children, Arvin, and possibly large amounts of evidence, we decided that we would fill them in on what was about to transpire the following morning.

14

Deliver Us From Evil

August 2, 1991

I didn't get much sleep the night before the raid. For several hours, I laid in bed staring at the ceiling, going over every detail of our plan. I glanced over at my wife as she slept soundly, wishing I could do the same. The house was so quiet I could hear my young children breathing in their sleep from across the hall. I dozed off briefly only to be awakened by a horrible nightmare of an armed confrontation with cult members and women and children running to escape. There was just no predicting the lengths these people would go to. Once my pulse slowed down, I realized nothing productive was going to happen while I stared at the ceiling listening to the faint tick of my alarm clock. At 2:45 am, I quietly slipped out of bed, showered, and dressed in the dark, and drove to my office to prep for the briefing that would begin at 4:00 am.

I don't remember much about the early morning drive except the streets were dark and nearly empty. The stoplights hanging above every other intersection of Washington Boulevard blinked their usual pattern of red, green, and amber but for no apparent reason. I stopped at every red light anyway.

I parked in the Municipal Building's nearly empty lot and entered the building through the back doors. I could feel my adrenalin kicking in as I made my way down the hollow and still hallway to my office. Turning on the light, I found the copies of the raid plans and assignments on my desk, just as I had left them. I grabbed the paperwork and made my way to the police briefing room. There I sat in silence for nearly an hour studying and memorizing every detail of our planned course of action.

Finally, the metal doors in the nearby locker room began clicking open and banging closed. Confused officers slowly filled the room. Several officers approached me and asked what was going on. I overheard some complaining about having to cancel personal plans. Most of the officers were annoyed that they hadn't been told much of anything. A few theorized they were being called to help with traffic control for a parade or special event of some kind.

When Sergeant Moore and Captain Balls entered the room, the grumblings stopped. As the chief of police and county attorney walked in, someone commented, "This is no Parade."

At precisely 4:00 am, Chief Empey welcomed the officers and social workers. Without introduction, he motioned to County Attorney Richards and me to address the group and make the assignments. I flipped on the overhead projector and displayed a map of the Northwood subdivision. Richards began the briefing by outlining the magnitude of the investigation and the need for secrecy. The message seemed to resonate with the officers, and their focus intensified.

For 60 minutes, we briefed, organized the search teams, and made assignments while answering questions. At 5:00 am, the officers were broken into their teams where they received additional instruction from their team leaders and gathered any extra equipment they would need. By 5:30 am, the teams were quietly heading to the staging area located just south of the subdivision. It was still dark when the patrol cars took their places. The cars' headlights were turned off and each officer sat waiting. Time flew as I moved from team to team to ensure search warrants were in hand.

At five minutes before the hour, the sun was barely beginning to brush the sky behind Ogden's east wall of mountains. The officers kept an eye on their watches as they ticked toward 6:00 am. At the assigned hour, Captain Balls radioed, "All units move in."

The teams inconspicuously sped to their assigned homes, and traffic control officers closed off the intersections into the neighborhood. Like precision clockwork, officers jumped from their cars and flooded the neighborhood. They simultaneously forced their way inside the front and rear entrances to the homes. In just three minutes, all teams reported their target home was secure, and all occupants were accounted for.

Our plans were pulled off flawlessly, and fortunately, none of the dangerous scenarios we had prepared for happened. The occupants of the homes were caught completely off guard and there were no altercations. Sergeant Moore's SWAT team was not needed. The raid was a success.

As groggy adults and children were being gathered in living rooms, I ran from house to house, looking for Arvin. His followers triumphantly reported he had left the area the day before, "proof he was inspired."

Within 30 minutes of beginning the raid, traffic control officers reported that crowds of media had arrived. Captain Balls began dealing with reporters who were trying to gain access to the crime scene.

The radio traffic was heavy and steady. Luckily, we were on a special radio channel that gave officers the luxury of sharing information without fighting for airtime with the patrol and detective divisions.

Detectives Bowcutt and Flink began systematically photographing the outside areas before moving inside the residences. As the operation progressed, the video and photographic evidence proved to be enormous and too much for two men to handle. Consequently, the collections process moved slowly.

The social workers were directed to enter the homes where children were waiting. They sensitively asked each child their name and prepared to take them into protective custody with the support of a police officer. This process was terribly difficult for everyone involved but was especially traumatic for the children. They didn't want to leave their familiar circumstances, regardless of what had happened to them there. Separating them from their abusers was difficult, and the effects would prove to be long-lasting. We knew this would be a problem, but there were just no other options. It was a lose-lose situation. Many of those officers who were on-scene that day will never forget the cries of the children still in their pajamas and clutching their scriptures as they were loaded into the Department of Family Services' vans, headed to foster homes and days of difficult interviews. As I watched the vans disappear down the street, I thought to myself, *I hope the children we are rescuing today are not the predators we jail tomorrow.*

Not being able to locate Arvin was a huge disappointment that was tempered by the victory of getting the children out of the reach of the predatory adults. I walked up and down the streets and through the yards hoping he would suddenly appear. I stopped in front of two of the homes we were not given permission to search and couldn't help wondering if he were peering out from behind the curtains of one of the windows.

15

Behind Closed Doors

The officers had a vague picture of what they were looking for during the raid, but none was quite prepared for the reality of what would be discovered. Many officers were astonished by the outside beauty of the homes. Detective Mark Acker, one of the team leaders, keenly observed, "These homes were not typical of those police officers are accustomed to being called to. They were well kept and decorated, comfortable looking dwellings. But the deeper we got into them the more contradictions arose."

. . .

"We mowed the lawns with push mowers—in two different directions. Once all the cutting and raking was done, we took a hose with a direct stream and squirted the entire space— including the grass—to remove any stitch of cut grass. We were trained to pick up any stray leaf when we saw it. Arvin required complete and total perfection at-all-times."

Andrea (age 16 at time of raid)

As I systematically moved through each home, investigators presented more information to me than any of us were prepared for. This was quickly becoming one of those "pay-days" that cops dream of. Each officer realized they were playing an essential role in the massive search warrant that would help end the long-term, horrific abuse of the cult's children. The officers immediately began uncovering key pieces of evidence that supported sexual abuse and exploitation. They were also being given a first-hand look into the inner workings of a cult. Most importantly, children were being rescued from the control of a deranged pedophile. As a result of the evidence being gathered, the self-proclaimed prophet and other culpable adults would be arrested. I felt immense satisfaction in the professional way each officer was carrying out their assignments.

The first home I approached was the cult's library. Detective Acker showed me into the basement where walls of bookshelves were filled with hundreds of books on various topics. The books were all cataloged in a similar manner to those in a public library. Acker pulled out a few books for evidence on disturbing subjects such as how to make false identification credentials, how to make bombs, a U.S. Army book on sniper tactics, martial arts books, and a book titled "Shooter's Bible." Just like in a library, check-out cards were included with the materials. Unfortunately, none of Arvin's personal writings were found here.

After reviewing the evidence, I hurried down the street to the home referred to as the dormitory for young girls. These girls were considered to be Arvin's "spiritual wives." This home was regarded as another perfect example of a Zion Home. It was called the "show house" because new recruits would be taken here to be shown an example of a "perfect" home.

Detective Mike Ashment came through the front door to meet me, "We found a lot of stuff Mike; you're not going to believe this place."

Ashment, who would later become the police chief, was a likable guy who wore western apparel. He was currently serving on the Narcotic Strike Force.

"They didn't need to damage any doors because one of the occupants opened them when the officers rang the doorbell," he said.

As we stepped inside, he pointed up the stairs to the main living area. "We've gathered the women and children together up there."

The home was a bi-level, split entry residence with a landing at the front door. Once inside, I paused long enough to look around. I couldn't help but notice that these walls were also covered with carpeting. I wondered what purpose this served. The tall wall to my left was oddly adorned with a headboard from a bed, fabric draped from each headpost. In the center of the "fixture" was a shelf holding a candle surrounded by artificial flowers. To the left of the candle, sat a picture of Jesus, and on the right stood a framed quote—"The motto of this home: To find the will of God in everything—and do it."

Ashment pointed to a wall switch at the side of the door.

"I wonder what this does," he said.

He flipped the switch up and a loud warbling alarm identical to the sound of emergency vehicles blared throughout the house. Amazed, he flipped it on and off a couple of times—just to assure himself it was real.

As we reached the top of the stairs, I saw the living room walls were also covered with carpeting. About 20 women and young girls were sitting quietly on a sofa and in chairs watching us. Still in their nightclothes, they had been given sheets and blankets to cover up. The expression on each face was oddly blank, emotionless.

Ashment and I walked past the silent spectators to the kitchen. The room was immaculate, not a dish or utensil to be seen. The cupboards held neatly stacked dishes and glassware. A large, black, wood-burning stove that appeared to be used for cooking stood prominently against one wall. Oddly, the room was decorated completely in pink. Pink cherry blossoms patterned the linoleum floor. The coordinating curtains and wallpaper were pink as well.

After taking in the living area and kitchen, Ashment and I headed down the hall toward the bedrooms. Again, the walls were covered with carpet. As we walked past the bathroom something caught my eye.

"Ashment," I said. "Look how perfectly these towels are hanging on this rack." I lifted the corner of one to examine it more closely. Each towel hung at exactly the same length, as if a ruler had been used for measuring. The color of the towels matched the color of the precisely folded washcloth that sat on the sink. Next to the washcloth was a soap dish that looked brand new, even though a half-used bar of soap sat in it. I pulled out the drawers of the cabinet and noticed various bathroom supplies arranged in an orderly manner. The toothbrushes were evenly lined up with all of the bristles facing the same direction. Everything, including the extra linen, was stacked uniformly.

> *"We would wake up at 7:30 am, make beds, bathe, comb hair, eat breakfast, do housework, meditate, study scriptures, sew, garden, clean again, bathe again, and go to bed at 9:30 pm."*
>
> Andrea

> *"I became a perfectionist out of fear–I was always fearful of making a mistake. I never felt I was good enough. When I was punished, I had to sit still for a half an hour and say nothing. I could not move except for my eyeballs."*
>
> Dawn (age 10 at time of raid)

> *"My days were not fun. I was being trained to be a 'spiritual' wife all the time. I was always being reprimanded for being too prideful."*
>
> Annessa (age 11 at time of raid)

> *"We were told we would go to hell if we weren't perfect. In reality, we were already living in hell."*
>
> Amber (escaped cult before raid)

Continuing down the hall, Ashment and I found each of the bedrooms to be decorated very femininely. Again, the walls were covered with carpeting. Other than the beds being unmade, due to the early morning raid, the rooms were orderly and immaculately clean.

Various religious pictures hung on the walls. One of the team members, Officer Blaine Clifford, was carefully inspecting dresser drawers in looking for evidence of crimes against children. He pointed out heaps of skimpy lingerie contained in some of the drawers. In others, he showed us stacks of neatly folded clothing, each topped with either a little bow or a tiny silk flower. The top drawer of a highboy dresser contained an envelope full of cash with the words, "Tithing for Arvin" handwritten across the top. Ashment opened the closet doors and discovered articles of clothing and shoes organized methodically according to color.

> *"We had to wear dresses or skirts all the time unless we were working in the yard. We were all assigned a color to wear. Mine was peach. I'd look in the closet and ask myself should I wear the peach dress or the peach dress or maybe the peach dress. To this day, I hate the color peach."*
>
> Amber

> *"Our clothes had to be suggestive in style. Whether it was tight skirts or low-cut blouses. Our gardening shorts were very short."*
>
> Andrea

"Have any weapons been found?" I asked
"Nothing yet," said Ashment.

I took Erin's hand-drawn map from my stack of papers and looked for the markings she had made indicating where hidden weapons could be found. When she served as Arvin's secretary, one of her responsibilities was to keep an inventory of the weapons and ammunition in each home. I repeatedly searched the exact locations Erin had marked on the map but could see no sign of weapons. Perplexed, I sat down on the bedroom floor with my back against the wall and continued to study the map. As I sat, I unconsciously pulled at the shag carpet with my fingers. The carpeting seemed to give way a little. I pulled at it again. The carpet was loose. I called for Ashment to come look as I tore the carpet up all the way to the corner of the room where it detached from the subfloor with the ripping sound of Velcro.

"No way," I said as I lifted a hinged floorboard revealing a hidden compartment below the subfloor. Inside were two fully loaded semi-automatic assault rifles.

Referring again to the map, Ashment and I headed to the master bedroom. "Ashment, it looks as though the reason for carpeting the walls is to conceal hidden compartments," I said. "It's the perfect camouflage for hidden access points." The map suddenly made more sense. Ashment went straight to the closet where he noticed belts hanging from a hook on the wall. When he pulled on the hook, a small piece of the wall opened to expose another compartment. This one contained a loaded revolver.

"Children were taken to a shooting range and taught to shoot and defend their homes for the end of the world."

Andrea

The basement of the home appeared ordinary with a large family room and a few small bedrooms. One bedroom contained children's bunkbeds. A small closet revealed a few baskets filled with toys. One of the investigators noticed a closet under the stairs. He opened it to find the walls were also completely covered in carpeting. The space seemed disproportionately small to the length of the stairs. He felt around the back wall and realized it was loose. He pushed and pulled until the wall opened, revealing a small dark compartment large enough to fit two or three people.

"The adults were obsessed with the book "The Hiding Place" by Corrie ten Boom. They had hidden rooms built in the houses that were soundproof. We were hidden in them when social services came around."

Amber

I left the dormitory house and headed directly across the street to the Sister Council house. This was where Arvin and his adult wives lived, including his legal wife, Alice. Detective John Stubbs, a very intense and excellent investigator, showed me around. The house was very similar in décor to the girls' dormitory. Again, the walls were covered with carpet. The living room, decorated entirely in baby blue, was immaculate. The kitchen seemed ordinary except for an oddly placed bathroom scale sitting on the floor.

> *"We were given a specific weight we were to maintain. We were weighed daily, and it was recorded on a chart. Carla and the other women would humiliate us in front of the others if we weighed too much."*
>
> Laura (age 18 at time of raid)

> *"I was told "God can't reach you through layers of fat," and that I wouldn't be wanted in a Sister Council until I lost weight."*
>
> Natalie

The bedrooms in this home were also decorated very femininely. The dresser drawers contained piles of women's stockings and lingerie all perfectly folded and stacked according to type, color, and size, similar to what one might see in a department store. All the rooms were very orderly except for the unmade beds. Stubbs opened the closet doors where, again, dresses all hung according to color and size. On the floor was a large shoe rack stacked full of women's high heels. He pulled on the rack to show me it was hinged to the subflooring. He rocked it backward to reveal a secret panel containing a Ruger Mini-14 assault rifle.

Stubbs then led me to the basement where we first entered a family room much like one in any ordinary home. The room held a sofa, a television, and a wood-burning stove. In one corner stood a desk and on it sat a few scattered pages of Arvin's ramblings, a stark reminder that this was no ordinary home. Down the hall were a couple of bedrooms.

One was unusually dark and dismal. Looking in, we saw that it was furnished very sparsely with only a bed. The walls were bare except for a cold air return vent.

When I returned outside, I stopped a moment to watch the social workers escorting the children into the DFS vans to be taken downtown to the Children's Justice Center. I noticed one of the teenage girls staring at me with contempt as she stepped into the van. Just then, a call came across my radio asking me to come to the home where Detective Casey Shorten was the lead investigator.

Shorten, an experienced officer in the department's Youth Bureau, walked me through each room of the home referred to as the storage house and motor pool. In the entry way of the home hung a small cabinet with various car keys. Each key was color-coded and marked with a number that corresponded with a chart hanging on the wall. The names of various members of the cult were recorded with the dates the vehicles had been checked out.

> *"We were taken on car rides to the country late at night. We had to do a strip tease dance in the car headlights and then we could go get ice cream for our reward."*
>
> Andrea

> *"Arvin took me for rides. He took me to Little Mountain and said he built it. He took me to the water tower at the Business Depot and he told me he built that too. To a 6-year-old girl with no steady father figure, he was mighty, and I believed him."*
>
> Kami (age 6 at time of raid)

Shorten led me to one of the bedroom closets and pointed to another hidden compartment. Opening a door concealed in the carpeted wall, he revealed two assault rifles.

I was taken down the stairs to the basement where Shorten's team had discovered a large storage room full of shelves stocked with over-the-counter and prescription drugs. The shelves were filled to capacity with hospital-sized containers stacked 24 to 36 bottles deep. The team photographed hundreds of bottles of prescription pills, later estimated by medical professionals to be worth more than $50,000. The prescriptions ranged from antibiotics to pain killers, and the medicines were supplemented by a large quantity of suture kits, bandages, and other medical supplies. Syringes, gynecological instruments, stethoscopes, and blood pressure cuffs were also found.

"Children were taken to the doctor for strep throat and were prescribed antibiotics, but they were never given the meds...the group stored them. After being seen by a doctor, members would steal as many medical supplies as they could hide in their bags and clothing. The teenage girls were required to visit the county health department using a fake name to get birth control pills."

Laura

Also found in the basement was a curious tiny room that had no lights or windows.

"We would be sent to a dark room with a pencil and paper. We were told to communicate with dead people (or guardian angels) and write down what they told us. We would ultimately make up people and things to write down to prove we connected with them. Arvin told us God was telling him what we were thinking and if we had done anything wrong. It was a frightening mind game."

Andrea

Detective Marcy Vaughn (Korgenski), a respected officer who would later become assistant chief, had a dignified and professional way about her. Detective Vaughn was assigned to lead the investigation at the home of one of the men in the cult and his wife. In this home, investigators found strange portals constructed in the walls making it possible to see from one room to another. There were also several air vents in the walls between rooms that seemed unnecessary except for possibly spying. Officers also found a secret gun portal that led to the outside of the house, cleverly camouflaged into the home's exterior.

Vaughn gathered the small family into the living room as investigators searched the home. The father was quiet and nonthreatening. The mother controlled her emotions and was courteous but obviously nervous as social workers gathered up their three children, aged seven, nine, and ten. The children were afraid and obviously upset. One was crying. As Vaughn and a social worker were gathering up items the children would need, they noticed the little ones had sores on their upper thighs.

"What are those sores on the children's thighs?" asked Vaughn.

"Oh, those are just hurps," said the mother.

Vaughn thought she heard "hurts" and said, "I know those are hurts but how did they get them?"

"They're just hurps," the mother repeated.

Vaughn then realized the mother was referring to "herpes" and was naïve to the seriousness of the disease.

Before relinquishing her children, the mother quietly asked if she could pray with them and was allowed to do so. After praying, the mother's demeanor changed, and she angrily declared she was going to protest the search warrant. The father remained seated, very quiet and unassuming. He was polite with the officers and even thanked them for being so professional.

The chatter on my police radio was constant as I rushed from house to house to see what the various teams had found. In every home, officers found box after box of home-bottled produce, canned food, boxes of processed meals, soaps, and paper goods. Basement rooms resembled warehouses with boxes of emergency supplies stacked to the ceiling.

I was most anxious to see what investigators had found at the home belonging to Arvin and Carla. This home was considered by group members to be almost sacred since they believed it was here that he received most of his "divine" inspiration.

I headed there to meet Detective Shane Minor who was leading the team investigating this house. He was an exceptional homicide investigator, who ultimately ended up working for the county attorney. Today, he'd been assigned to lead the investigation of the most disturbing house in the commune.

Police officers learn early in their careers to tuck their emotions away when investigating violent crimes, especially those involving children. Today, this was nearly impossible to carry out. As I watched the children being escorted to the vans, I couldn't help but think of my own kids who were similar in age. As a father, I couldn't imagine allowing something this horrific to have happened to them. Regardless of my training and conditioning, I felt outrage as I approached the lynch-pin's residence.

As Minor showed me around, I couldn't help but feel sickened knowing the criminal acts that were alleged to have taken place here. Aside from a few subtle differences between this home and the others, the furnishings, the décor, and the orderliness were boringly similar. Just like the other homes, religious pictures hung on carpet-covered walls.

I felt uneasy as we entered the master bedroom. This was one of two rooms in which Arvin and Carla carried out their despicable acts. The room was decorated with bright fuchsia and pink colors. A quaint five-inch pink ruffle hung all around the room at the top of the walls. A flouncy, floral bedspread covered the king-sized bed that Arvin and Carla shared. It was undisturbed. Lace curtains hung over the windows. On the wall next to the bed was what appeared to be a light switch. Minor flipped it, and a deafening siren echoed throughout the house and beyond. Investigators recovered a number of sex devices and instructional manuals. One device was lying on top of an open Bible.

"I remember he smelled of sweat, freshly cut grass, and dirt. After he had his way with me, I had to stay in bed with Arvin all night, but I couldn't sleep. I would stare out the window through the lace curtains."

Amber

"Arvin told us sex was how he bonded with young girls."

Dawn

"Arvin told us that his "heavenly spirit" was much younger than his earthly body and our "heavenly spirits" were older than our earthly bodies. It was his way of justifying the huge age difference between the young girls and himself."

Amber

"We were told we couldn't go to heaven unless we had sex with Arvin."

Andrea

"Arvin's legal wife, Alice, would prepare us for our encounters with him. She would give us treats and calmly explain what was going to happen so we wouldn't be afraid."

Amber

This was the home where Carla taught the Sexual Way of Life to the children. It was also in this home that Rape in the Dark and other sex games were played on a regular basis. Here we discovered the instructional manuals created by Arvin and Carla, including The Sexual Way of Life. We also found the many bogus "revelations" Arvin claimed to have received, all organized in three-ring binders.

"Carla taught us the sexual way of life. She was the sexual expert. She invented the Rape in the Dark Game. We were terrified of her. The older girls had to teach the younger girls how to be the sexual aggressors and how to seduce Arvin."

Annessa

The cult referred to this home as the "beautification home." The name became apparent when we entered a large room in the basement that served as the sewing headquarters for the "Sweet Things" lingerie business. The room was filled with sewing machines and the walls were lined with pink, hand-sewn curtains that concealed walls of shelves stacked with fabric and notions. Shelves and closets held skimpy, homemade lingerie. In one corner was a sink and mirror for coloring, cutting, or perming hair. It was in this room that the girls were primped, preened, and readied to seductively model for strangers or to seduce Arvin.

"We had to look perfect every day. Our hair was perfect, our clothes were perfect, and so was our make-up. Even little girls were taught how to apply makeup."

Amber

By lunchtime, each of the homes we had search warrants for had been thoroughly inspected. Detective Lucas had collected a huge amount of evidence from the officers in each home. Detectives Bowcutt and Flink had burned through dozens of rolls of film, documenting the contents of each room including the location of hidden firearms and pornography. By chance, Detective Flink photographed one of the most important pieces of evidence in the case. At the home that served as the dormitory for the adult women, his photograph captured the air vent between a crawl space into the small, dark room in the Sister Council house. Later testimony would uncover that a little girl had hid in the small space and watched through the vent as Arvin brought a young boy into the small room and sexually assaulted him.

At the end of the day, all the officers were curious about the backyard bunker. Because Erin was unable to give us any information about its purpose or contents, we had not been able to get a warrant to search it. The homeowner was, not surprisingly, less than cooperative when I asked him, "Is Arvin inside that fortress?" I would never find out for certain if he was or not, but some of the cult members later said that he had been inside throughout the raid.

As the day came to a close and the evidence was removed, we realized that we had missed breakfast and lunch, and there were still hours of reports to be written. The mental health providers reported back that the children had been placed into protective custody and were being scheduled for interviews. Some were already underway. The amount of work involved in this case was proving to be staggering.

OPD 91-13795
8/2/91

SISTER COUNCIL RESIDENCE
NORTHWEST BEDROOM

OPD 91-13795
8/2/91

ENTRYWAY TO
CHILDREN'S DORM

Source: Ogden City, Utah Police Department Raid Photo, Technical Services

OPD 91-13795
8/2/91

RUGER MINI-14
ASSAULT RIFLE,
CHILDREN'S DORMITORY
UPSTAIRS S/W ROOM

OPD 91-13795
8/2/91

REVOLVER IN
HIDDEN COMPARTMENT
CHILDREN'S DORMITORY
UPSTAIRS N/W BDRM

OPD 91-13795
8/2/91

ARVIN'S HOUSE
BASEMENT ROOM

OPD 91-13795
8/2/91

CHILDREN'S DORMITORY
HIDING SPOT

Source: Ogden City, Utah Police Department Raid Photo, Technical Services

PRESCRIPTION DRUGS, MEDICAL FACILITY
OPD 91-13795 8/2/91

CANNED FOOD STORAGE

FOOD STORAGE IN BASEMENT OF LIBRARY
OPD 91-13795 8/2/91

Source: Ogden City, Utah Police Department Raid Photo, Technical Services

PART THREE

"We didn't know it was wrong
until you told us it was."
                              Victims

16

The Devil's Dolls

Once the raid was completed, the social workers escorted the children and their mothers downtown to the newly constructed Children's Justice Center (CJC). The scene was extremely emotional. The little ones were frightened and crying. The older children were angry and defiant. Once inside the center, the mothers were separated from their children to insure they didn't influence their child's testimony. Because of the extensive work that was ahead of the social workers, a few volunteers were asked to help busy the children as they waited to be interviewed. The very affable Joan Hellstrom was a county commissioner at the time. She chipped in by helping the young girls bake cookies in the center. Such activities were helping to calm the children and the social workers were grateful for the support as they were exhausted with the enormity of the day's work. With only a few hours of preparation, they'd been required to rely on their combined experience to evaluate and adjust an ongoing interview strategy. Experienced and competent, they possessed a cadre of multi-disciplinarian professionals to back them up. However, this situation was unique. Not only would they be conducting multiple interviews with the children, but also, in a number of cases, several members of the same family would need to be interviewed. The logistics were overwhelming.

The team was informed that the children had been coached in how they should respond to police and social workers' questions. Team members even overheard the older children instructing the younger ones not to say anything. The team realized it would be a challenge to assess the children's truthfulness and the accuracy of their statements.

In some of the cases involving very young children, the child's mother was allowed to come to the center while their child was being interviewed. However, the mothers were not allowed to sit in on the interview. The team hoped that having the mother present would lead the child to feel that their parent was supportive of the interview process. It was also hoped that the mother's presence would have a calming effect on the child being interviewed.

As CJC personnel worked through the scheduling and developed their game plan, the children were being dressed and fed at their respective foster homes. Seven blocks from the CJC, the staff in the county attorney's office was fielding calls from the distraught parents and their lawyers, demanding the return of the children. The media was in a frenzy, attempting to get information, statements, and on-camera interviews. News outlets from as far away as Los Angeles crowded hallways in the municipal building and scoured the Northwood Subdivision.

While all the commotion was taking place, I sat impatiently in the waiting area of the district court. I had arrived early in hopes I would catch Judge West and provide him with the "Return of Search Warrant" as he arrived for work. I continued to check my watch, pacing the floor as I waited. There was so much to do. The judge arrived shortly before nine and invited me into his office. I presented the documents to him, and as he flipped through the pages, he said, "You had a busy day." Satisfied that everything was in order, the judge accepted the return and dismissed me.

Arriving at the CJC just moments after the first interview began, I slipped into one of the adjacent rooms to observe through closed-circuit TV. I watched with interest as Jan and Laura worked to build a rapport with the child being interviewed.

As I adjusted the volume on the television, I heard Jan say, "I don't know the answers to the questions I am going to ask you. Would you please help me understand everything in your own words? You can tell me if I'm wrong or if I make a mistake."

The child nodded.

"What would you say if I asked if you were 30 years old?"

"I'm only nine," the child said with a smile.

And with that type of exchange, the children began to relax and open up. The interviews lasted long enough to get as much information as possible but were promptly concluded when it became apparent when they were becoming overly taxing for the child. The interviews took place over a couple of days, and as time passed, Jan's rapport with the children increased. Slowly, the children gained trust in the social workers and began to share crucial information.

The children related details of systemic abuses by Arvin and the women in his Sister Council that occurred almost daily over a period of years. The girls explained continual efforts made by the older women in the group to sexualize them. As if it were a normal educational exercise, older girls were directed to compile a scrapbook displaying what they thought were representations of their sexual nature. The compilations the girls put together included various clothing and hairstyles. They were told that once they came to an understanding of their nature, other girls will come seeking the secrets of their beauty. The children were also trained in sexuality using pornographic visual aids. Children said they were forced to watch adults in the group engage in sexual activities. One child disclosed that Carla had taken naked pictures of the children and had given them to Arvin. Another child stated that other men in the group besides Arvin also sexually abused the young boys.

Detective Lucas and I watched most of the interviews, but one in particular remained in my memory for years. Jan and Laura were interviewing a child about some physical injuries that she was found to have. The child confided that she was assaulted many times by the adult women in the group. The women forced the girl to satisfy their sexual demands. She stated that the first time she was assaulted was around the time she turned seven years old. She said she remembered it because, "it scared me and stuck out in my mind." She added that most of the assaults occurred in the afternoon. She also accused Arvin of raping her, and she described his body in detail. Lucas and I sat speechless as that little girl talked. *How could anyone do such a horrendous thing? Even worse, how could someone justify such an atrocity in the name of spirituality?* It was horrifying. The little girl's testimony was convincing and powerful when coupled with the physical trauma she endured.

Between the assaults by the women and the rapes by Arvin, there was enough testimony and physical evidence to add these assaults to the growing list of violent felonies committed by adult cult members. We would later learn from adult members' confessions that this child was only six years old when the sexual assaults began. She alone was probably victimized over 300 times by at least six adults, including Arvin. As the interviews progressed, the children repeated similar scenarios over and over.

While the children were being interviewed, I would watch and wait for the parents to come in for a visitation with their child. I would invite the parents to speak to me, but most declined. Those who did agree gave carefully rehearsed responses to my questions, leaving me frustrated. I knew they were lying.

Upon hearing that his young daughter divulged that she had been sexually abused by the women and raped by Arvin multiple times, one father became angry and retorted, "We are too good of friends to our children to be unaware of this." The mother then piped in, "I have a psychology background from college, and you don't know what you are talking about." To avoid escalation, I transitioned my questions to the disturbing sexual teachings inside the cult and asked, "What can you tell me about the Sister Councils?" Both parents said they had heard of the concept but had no knowledge of it being practiced. They went on to say that they whole-heartedly believed in Arvin's teachings, and felt that Sister Councils were divinely inspired. They quickly added, "But we don't feel that we personally are spiritual enough to enjoy the blessings of those teachings."

I looked at the mother and asked pointedly,

"Why do you think they are teaching The Sexual Way of Life to the children inside the homeschool you call, The Midland Academy?"

"The students in the Midland Academy are surpassing students in the public education system *(Not according to district personnel[1])*," she stated proudly. "All of the children are required to pass each course with 100% accuracy, even though our instructors are not certified teachers," she said, evading my question.

The parents then began accusing me of "thrashing their belief system" and refused to talk any further. They had said enough.

During the interviews, the children openly admitted that the adults had done sexual things to them. Still, they refused to show any of the things that happened using the CJC's anatomically correct dolls. It seemed the children were horrified by the dolls, mentally and emotionally "shutting down" when the dolls were brought into the room. The interviews would come to a screeching halt when the dolls were brought out.

Puzzled, we opted to set up a more in-depth interview with the professional social workers at nearby Primary Children's Hospital. The professionals specialized specifically in child sexual abuse. Fortunately, upon hearing the circumstances, the respected forensic psychologist Dr. Kevin J. Gully cleared his teaching calendar at the University of Utah and agreed to conduct the interviews the following day.

After meeting with the children, Dr. Gulley reported that he found the children to be alert and coherent and that they demonstrated they were not influenced by any "leading test questions." At the conclusion of the interviews, he determined the children truthfully described the sexual assaults they had been subjected to and identified the people who had assaulted them. He noted the children demonstrated the ability to provide factual information while possessing a moral duty to tell the truth. The doctor believed the children suffered from Post-Traumatic Stress Disorder but were capable of providing testimony in court.

I called Erin to ask if she knew why the children would respond so negatively to the dolls.

"Wow. It really worked," she said. "Several months before I left the group, an ex-husband of one of the cult women showed up and demanded to see his children. It was a chaotic situation, and one of the neighbors must have called the police. The man was ordered to leave the area. Shortly afterward, Arvin told us he'd received inspiration that the police were going to raid the houses and that we needed to destroy all of the pornography. We were burning stuff and hiding things that he thought would be a problem. Members of the group were moving things from their houses to their cars and taking items to storage areas. But the raid never happened."

Erin said even though there was no raid, Arvin's paranoia only intensified. He became convinced each unrecognizable car driving through the neighborhood or any unfamiliar person walking a dog was an undercover police officer trying to obtain intelligence on the group. Arvin also realized the ever-present threat that other disgruntled ex-spouses or nosey neighbors could call police again. He assembled the men together to develop an anti-interrogation seminar designed to teach the adults and, ultimately, the children how to respond to police or social workers if they were ever interviewed.

"The men began holding training sessions with the women and children. They would dress up like police officers and question the children about the members of the group, the cult and its beliefs, and, most importantly, about sexual things. The children were taught how to answer questions and lie about the things that were going on. They were warned that they would go to hell if they ever told anyone."

Erin said Carla had obtained two anatomically correct dolls. She knew law enforcement and mental health professionals were using the dolls to help children act out experiences, so she began using the dolls as a tool to frighten the children. She told them the dolls were tools of the devil, and they were never to look at or touch the evil dolls. The children's reactions in Dr. Gulley's interviews now made sense.

17

Taking the Bait

August 5, 1991

Three days after the raid, Detective Lucas and I sat in a concealed room at the Children's Justice Center watching interviews of children from the Zion Society. Suddenly, my pager went off, showing "911" on the message screen. This was a code from the county attorney's office telling me I needed to call them immediately.

When I did, the first words out of the secretary's mouth were, "Cedar City Police have Arvin in custody."

I couldn't believe my ears. "Are you sure? How did they get him?" I asked.

Lucas jumped to his feet. I held up my hand to motion him to hold on while I gathered more information.

I finished the call and burst out, "He turned himself in, Lucas! The bounder walked into the Cedar City Police Department and told them we were looking for him."

I immediately called the Cedar City department and was told they could detain Arvin for up to eight hours in their holding cells, but we needed to get there as soon as possible.

"Do not ask him any questions. We are on our way. Don't tell the press," I said.

We quickly made arrangements to make the 300 miles trip south to Cedar City. We were assigned a yellow Chevy Camaro T-top vehicle that had been part of an undercover drug operation. And it was fast.

Lucas and I jumped in the car and headed to the county shops to gas up and grab enough Diet Coke to make the long drive. We planned to use the drive to fine-tune our interview strategy in hopes that Arvin would agree to talk to us.

Once we left the Wasatch Front metropolitan area, we were driving in a rather remote part of the state landscaped with scenic desert mountains and fields of sagebrush. Since there were few cars on the freeway, I decided to take advantage of the sports car's abilities and "stepped on the gas." As we sped down the road, we caught the attention of a highway patrol trooper traveling in the opposite direction and running radar. The officer turned on his lights and headed toward a barrow pit to make a U-turn, obviously intending to pull us over. I put my foot to the floor, watching through my rear-view mirror as the trooper's car fell further behind us.

Lucas started laughing. "Hey buddy, you might want to call the highway patrol dispatch."

"You're right," I said and radioed the dispatch to explain the situation. Then I slowed the car until the trooper could catch up with us. As he pulled alongside our car, Lucas held up his badge. The trooper immediately turned off his lights and waved us on. Thankfully, the dispatcher made a point of calling ahead to the troopers along Interstate 15 to alert them we would be passing through.

Lucas and I sat quietly as we got closer to our destination—both of us feeling the tension of what we were about to encounter. As the passing fields of sagebrush turned into hills of Juniper trees, Lucas finally broke the silence. "You know, Cedar City should have probably been named Juniper City," he said, "but the early pioneers mistook the junipers for cedar trees." I smiled courteously. We slowed down to take the first exit into the small town and with our arrest plan in place and time to spare, we pulled into the Cedar City Police Department.

The police chief met us at the door. "Your guy is in the back waiting for you," he said with a smile. "He just walked in this morning and said, 'the Ogden Police Department is looking for me.' He said he had been traveling between Arizona and Nevada when a friend told him there was a warrant out for his arrest. He said he hitched a ride here."

The chief confirmed that Arvin had said nothing else and then escorted us to the holding area. I was extremely anxious to meet the notorious pedophile, but I was taken aback by the man I saw when I walked toward the cell. This man who reigned over more than a hundred people and convinced them he was speaking for God while he sexually abused children was extraordinarily ordinary. At sixty-one years of age, Arvin looked older. He was dressed dowdily in what looked like an inexpensive pair of khaki slacks that fell below his bulging waistline. He was also wearing a nondescript short-sleeved blue shirt and large square-framed glasses. His thinning hair was turning gray. He resembled any typical grandfather.

As we entered the room, Arvin struggled to stand, impeded by the restraints he was wearing. He reached out his cuffed hands and politely said, "Hello, I'm Arvin." He then became oddly conversational. "I'm sorry you had to travel so far to speak to me," he continued. "The moment I heard police were looking for me, I turned myself in. How are the children?" he finished in a soft, concerned tone.

"The children are doing well. We've been interviewing them for the past three days, and we're learning a lot. In fact, we would like to ask you some questions," I said.

Arvin looked at me suspiciously and then responded with his gentlemanly charm, "I'd be happy to help clear up this misunderstanding."

"Arvin, I need you to understand that we are placing you under arrest for sexual abuse of a child. Before we start asking you some questions, I need to advise you of your rights."

Arvin assumed a stunned expression as if he were having a hard time comprehending what was happening. We weren't falling for his disingenuous act.

I read him his rights and asked, "Do you understand each of these rights I have explained to you?"

He thought for a few moments and then said, "Yes."

My heart was thumping so hard in my chest that I feared its beating might be visible as I continued, "Having these rights in mind, do you wish to talk to us now?"

In one of the most disheartening moments in my career he said, "No, I better talk with an attorney first."

I tried not to show my disappointment.

"Great," I said. "Let's jump in the car and head back to Ogden where we will book you into the Weber County Jail. There, you'll be able to reach out to your legal representative." I placed a call to Richards to inform him that Arvin had asked for an attorney. He suggested we use the ride home to talk about inconsequential things and hope Arvin would slip up.

And with that, Detective Lucas and I transferred custody of Arvin from the Cedar City Police Department into our safekeeping. We placed him in a belt with handcuffs and ankle shackles. As Arvin hobbled to the car with Lucas, I finalized the paperwork.

Lucas tilted the front seat forward in the Camaro and had Arvin crawl into the back seat. Luckily, Arvin was short enough to fit into the small space. Lucas fastened Arvin's seatbelt, proceeded to the front of the car, and sat down in the front passenger seat.

"You put the old guy in the back seat?" I asked, quietly chuckling as I got into the driver's seat.

"Well, *I* certainly wasn't going to ride back there all the way home," said Lucas.

We started the long ride back to Ogden at about four o'clock in the afternoon. Now that Arvin had asked for an attorney, we initiated our backup plan. Since Arvin was such an "authority" on God and scripture, we planned to goad him by discussing religion on the entire drive back to Ogden.

At the time, Lucas and I were both serving in leadership positions in our local church which happened to be the same church Arvin had been excommunicated from. We knew our conversation would pique his interest.

Lucas started the conversation, asking, "How are you enjoying your church assignment, Mike?"

"I'm enjoying it, but I do get frustrated when the elders don't do their visits. They will look you right in the eye and tell you they are doing them when they aren't. I don't know how to motivate them."

"Are you holding interviews with them?" Lucas asked.

"Yes, but I guess I just don't know the right things to say."

When I glanced in the rearview mirror, I saw that Arvin was listening closely. The eyes behind his signature glasses were shifting back and forth, first on me, then on Lucas. He reminded me of a wary trout darting toward a hook and then turning away before spinning around and finally taking the bait. I was hoping Arvin would take the bait.

The conversation continued as we talked about faith, philosophy, and church doctrine. We didn't really have a script. And then we hit a nerve.

"Dave, how do you deal with people in your congregation who quit coming to church?" I asked.

Arvin couldn't stand it any longer. He had to chime in.

"You keep trying and hoping," he said. "You need to understand where they are. It's like those of us who live by each other in Ogden. We're just friends and neighbors who help each other. Nothing more."

"Arvin, we can't talk to you about this. You've asked for an attorney," I said, stopping him.

"This is a gospel discussion, and it doesn't have anything to do with what you've charged me with," he said.

We remained adamant that Arvin couldn't speak to us, and he leaned back in his seat, deflated.

When we neared the small town of Nephi, I looked at my watch and commented that it was taking an unusually long time to get to Ogden. We decided to stop and have some dinner.

As we pulled into a truck-stop diner, I asked Arvin if he would be comfortable going into the restaurant and sitting down to eat.

"We can put a jacket over your handcuffs and remove the leg shackles if you'll promise to behave."

He promised and thanked us for allowing him to stretch.

"Sorry about the backseat," I said.

We walked up to the diner entrance, and I peered through the windows. I saw there were only a few customers inside. I walked in while Lucas kept Arvin outside. I asked to speak with the manager and requested a table in the back of the room. The manager graciously complied, and I returned to help Lucas escort Arvin inside. I asked Lucas how he felt about us removing the handcuffs so that Arvin wouldn't be embarrassed. He agreed and we removed the cuffs.

"Don't do anything stupid, Arvin," I said.

He promised that he would do everything we asked and thanked us for our "kindly consideration."

The waitress came to our table and placed a glass of water in front of each of us. Then she briskly passed us each a menu. Without thinking I said, "One bill please. For the two of us and my dad."

Lucas looked surprised and tried not to laugh.

"You got it," the waitress said and walked away.

Arvin didn't say a word, but I noticed a few tears in his eyes.

"You are the nicest guys," he said. "Thank you for treating me so kindly. I really want to tell you about the neighborhood I live in."

Did he think he was going to convert us?

We reminded him that we couldn't talk to him because he had demanded an attorney. And for the next hour, the three of us ate together while Arvin listened to Lucas and me chat about religion again.

All this talk was clearly having an effect on Arvin because once we got on the road again, he reiterated he wanted to talk. Again, we refused. After another 40 minutes of listening to us talk about religion, Arvin demanded that we get his lawyer on the phone. He told us he wanted to waive his right and talk to us.

Using one of the early models of mobile phones, we tried for nearly an hour to reach Arvin's attorney. We called the lawyer's office and his home. We even had officers go to his home, but no luck. As we neared Ogden and the Weber County Jail, Arvin demanded to talk.

Lucas notified the dispatcher we would be arriving soon and asked that the jail be alerted. The dispatcher told us news had gotten out that Arvin was in custody, and there was a huge gathering of press outside the building.

As we were stopped at a red light in front of the Utah Highway Patrol offices in the Ogden suburb of South Ogden, Arvin became agitated.

"I want to fire my attorney," he said.

He took the bait!

"Pull over Mike," Lucas said. "I think we should stop here and interview him."

I pulled into the parking lot, turned in my seat, and reminded Arvin of the charges he was facing.

"Are you sure you want to do this, Arvin?" I asked.

"Yes, I do, and right now," he asserted.

18

Lies and Confessions

Lucas called the dispatch office on our mobile phone so our location wouldn't be broadcast across the airwaves that are monitored by the press and inquisitive citizens. He let them know the situation—that Arvin had waived his rights to an attorney, and we were going to interrogate him.

The bright orange sun could be seen reflecting off the Great Salt Lake as we drove into the parking lot of the Highway Patrol office. It wasn't long before Sergeant Ted McGregor pulled up and let us in the small building that doubled as the office of the Department of Motor Vehicles. We requested a tape recorder and asked McGregor to stay in the room as a witness to Arvin waiving his rights to counsel.

There we were, King, Lucas, McGregor, and Arvin, sitting around a table just a few miles from the jail. Lucas re-Mirandized Arvin and, one by one, he waived each right.

"Arvin, are you under any duress or force to do this?" asked Sgt. McGregor.

"No."

And with that, we began interrogating the cult leader.

As with all my interviews, I began by reflecting on an old adage by Abraham Maslow: *He who is good with a hammer thinks everything is a nail.* Just because a certain strategy works on one type of offender doesn't mean it will work on the next. I knew flexibility would be the key to this interrogation.

One of my strategies was to create a relationship of understanding with Arvin. It was very important that I not convey a judgmental attitude while still remaining skeptical. I began by asking him questions that I knew would solicit truthful responses. I asked about his childhood, his family, and his passion for landscaping. I tried to appear interested and impressed with his skills. As he answered, I focused on his behavior. Unbeknownst to Arvin, I was constructing a mental truth detector I could subsequently use against him. As I listened to him speak about inconsequential and nonthreatening topics, I busily made notes of his nonverbal cues. Without knowing, Arvin was teaching me how to recognize whether he was telling the truth or not by the changes in his facial expressions and body language.

After the small talk, I shifted the line of questioning abruptly.

"Have you ever been arrested?"

"No," he said as if offended.

I tried not to smile as I was making mental notes of the cues I had just observed. The twitching in Arvin's neck and the shifting of his eyes revealed his discomfort as he answered. These signals revealed he was lying, and I now knew the interview and interrogation process would be much more efficient than anticipated.

"Arvin, I know that talking about the inappropriate things from your past may be difficult for you, but you need to know that I've spent an awful lot of time learning everything there is to know about you. Heck, I might even know more about you than you know about yourself. Now, you need to understand that I really want to throw the book at you for abusing those kids. Still, the county attorney thinks you deserve a chance to explain what happened in order to help us understand the circumstances better and get the children any help they may need. I'm going to give you only one example of how much I know about you and then we're going to start talking again. If you tell me the truth, I will make sure the court knows that you accepted responsibility for any wrongdoing, but, if you lie to me one more time, I'm going to do everything in my power to make sure you die in prison. Do you understand me?"

I leaned in closer and said, "Arvin, I know that you were arrested for soliciting sex workers. In fact, I spoke with Melanie, who told me about the time you told her that you wished you had a place where you could live with her and the other prostitutes she works with and protect them."

In a rare moment, he dropped his head and he looked at the floor. There was silence. Then, as if a lightbulb had turned on inside his brain, he looked up.

In a calm tone he said, "My wife and I discussed hiring a prostitute. I told her God had directed me to do it in order to gain additional knowledge regarding sexual things. She felt it was the right thing to do and encouraged it. I only did it a few times."

I leaned back in my chair.

"Only a few times?"

"I don't know exactly how many times it happened, and it was over a three-year period of time. I don't remember this prostitute named Melanie though. I want you to know that I often wished that God would have told me to do something other than that, but I will do anything for God," was his outrageous answer.

I shifted to less threatening questions.

"Tell me about the neighborhood you live in and the people you associate with," I said.

It was obvious he had thought this answer through many times before. He detailed how the group came together as friends who were trying to help each other.

"We all have a love of gardening," he said. "At their request, I would help them."

He went on to claim he didn't know the neighbors very well and pretended to struggle with names. His body language, however said something different, ratting him out once again. His jugular vein throbbed as he tried to keep direct eye contact with me.

"Are you the leader of a religious group of people?" I asked.

"I have some friends in the neighborhood who get together to study the scriptures, that's all," he replied.

"I don't get it, Arvin. Everyone I've questioned out there speaks about you with a certain amount of reverence, even referring to you as the patriarch of the neighborhood or a spiritual leader."

"I would never consider myself to be a spiritual leader, just a friend."

His jugular throbbed harder. Gotcha Arvin.

"It makes me wonder though. During the search, we recovered a stack of money that was in an envelope marked, 'Tithing for Arvin.' Can you explain that?"

He pursed his lips and smiled his trademark smile. "Someone must have been making a joke," he said.

It was time to begin interrogating Arvin on the charges of child sexual abuse. I reached into my briefcase and pulled out a stack of file folders and placed them on the table.

"Arvin, we have been very busy in the last week interviewing the children from your neighborhood. I want you to know that we have overwhelming evidence against you, enough to put you in prison for the rest of your life."

I paused and watched him closely. Lucas then set out to persuade him to confess.

"What we're trying to do here Arvin, is give you a chance to show the judge who you really are," Lucas said. "Now's the time to tell the truth. The judge would much rather hear everything from you."

We both stopped talking and waited.

And then it happened. In his holier than thou demeanor, Arvin began. "My understanding of the offense you are charging me with is that of illegal sexual contact with children. May I emphasize from the beginning that there was never any element of force, coercion, or persuasion. All contact was initiated by the children in a very natural and casual manner. I am definitely not implying some blame on the part of the children, nor attempting to mitigate any responsibility on my part as an adult. I simply wish the facts to be known. The purpose of such contact was not lust or sexual gratification but bonding and the building of a closeness within what was perceived as an eternal family unit. I realize that such is outside the norm of society's accepted standards. I realize also that due to the tendency that some in society have to abuse children or use them for personal gratification that laws must be formed to protect children from such behavior. However, my actions are perceived, I recognize that I am subject to such laws. I deeply regret my actions."

"When and how did all this begin, Arvin?" I asked.

He paused. We waited again.

He then went into a lengthy story of his very personal descent from his faith. He confessed he had suffered overwhelming guilt at that long-ago meeting with his church leaders. He said that after he denounced his church and left the meeting, he called back, asking to be forgiven, and was granted another interview later that same night. Unfortunately, he said he became angry again and re-affirmed his disbeliefs to his church leaders. "I didn't trust them," he said. "I got up and walked out of the church and never returned."

In one of the most theatrical moments of our interview, Arvin said, "After returning home from that ugly meeting, I felt extreme darkness around me. I acknowledged that I had lost the light of Christ. I could physically feel the emptiness. So, I was willing to accept any spirit, even an evil one, to fill the void."

"Arvin, are you trying to tell us that the devil made you do it?" I asked.

Arvin began to backpedal. "What I'm telling you is that later that night I had a dream, and in that dream, I was visited by a man who told me that if I deny Christ again, I would never have another chance at forgiveness. It scared me. And for that reason, I have never attempted to return to church. You might ask why, Mike. The answer is simple. I am unsure what answer I may give if asked those same questions again."

Proud of his explanation, he folded his arms across his chest and rocked back in his chair. "If the Church wants to find me, they know where to look."

It became apparent to me that Arvin housed a great deal of guilt about the perversions he was embracing during that time in his life including his pornography addiction and his involvement with sex workers. By shifting the blame of his mistakes to his church leaders, he somehow felt justification for his actions.

And then, in what seemed like a desperate move, Arvin attempted to protect the other culpable adults. "I also want you to know that I wasn't totally truthful about my friends in the neighborhood. We were close but they were not involved in any of this. I acted alone. Some of them knew about my belief in heavenly families but it wasn't generally known by those with whom I associated. In other words, there were varying degrees of knowledge or even beliefs in a plural marriage system. While religious in nature, it was based on a very close neighborhood relationship of unity and cooperation. My best description is that we were a diligent religious community."

It was clear Arvin had a reservoir of lies and deceptions. It was time now to talk about the charges. I walked through each child's accusation, one by one. After hearing each child's name and the details of the assaults, Arvin blamed the child. With one particular victim, he said, "Yes, that is possible. She was 'risky' in her actions. She seemed to encourage the contact." He then detailed his assault on the girl and tried to justify the assault as bonding.

The blame game continued as we talked about his assaults on ten other victims. We now had confessions to 30 felony sex abuse charges although he would never admit to any assaults on boys.

Completely disgusted and exhausted, we wrapped up the interrogation.

"Arvin, how often did this kind of thing happen?" was my final question.

"It was a daily thing," he began. "If I asked you what you had for breakfast last week on Thursday, you wouldn't know. You would know that you had breakfast, just not what and where," was his revolting answer.

It was midnight and we had been interrogating Arvin for more than three hours. We finally made our way to the jail and drove the Camaro across the grass and sidewalk to the front doors. Even with the late hour, throngs of shouting reporters and blinding flashbulbs greeted us. We hurried Arvin into the building, and he was booked into jail. Lucas and I snuck out the back doors to our cars and headed home to get a few hours of sleep.

Arvin's Arrest. Source: KTVX Salt Lake City, Utah

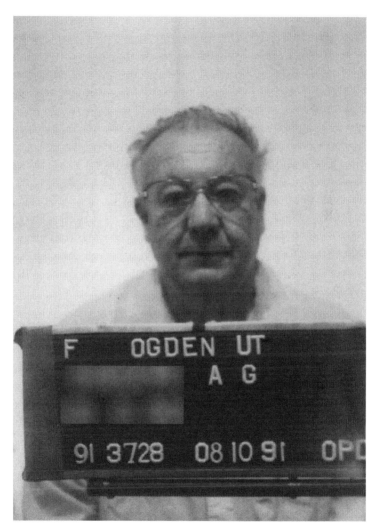

Arvin's Booking
Source: Weber County Utah
Department of Corrections

19

The Floodgates Open

After a few short hours of sleep, I met with Richards early the next morning. I brought him up to speed on Arvin's confession while we prepared for the arraignment, which was scheduled to begin in a couple of hours. In fewer than five weeks, we had moved the case from discovery to prosecution. The situation wasn't the norm. Such quick progress was only made possible because dozens of police officers, social workers, and prosecutors worked tirelessly and selflessly toward the common goal of rescuing abused children.

Even though Arvin had confessed to nearly 30 counts of child sexual abuse, we realized there was no guarantee the charges would stick. For one thing, we felt it likely that Arvin's attorney would challenge the waiver of his Miranda Rights. Richards felt we could overcome that since Arvin, himself, had demanded the waiver. We also had several independent witnesses to the formal refusal of his rights, strengthening our position.

Richards decided to file only four charges against Arvin and purposely excluded the allegations of abuse on the young boys. For some reason, Arvin continued to deny abusing the boys, and we knew he would fight the charges. I surmised that his concocted religion only allowed sex with "spiritual wives," whether young or old, and even he knew he had overstepped his own perverted doctrine. Instead, Richards opted to file charges that we believed Arvin would find more palatable, the rape of the young girls. *As if such an atrocity could be considered palatable by any human being with a conscience.* Richards strategically held the other criminal counts as leverage, knowing Arvin faced life in prison either way. He was prepared to formally charge the pedophile with two counts of sodomy on a child and two counts of sexual abuse of a child.

When we left Richard's office, we were confronted by hordes of people crowding the noisy hallway. Winding our way through a mob of reporters and photographers clamoring for a sound bite, Richards and I made our way into the packed and stuffy courtroom. Benches resembling church pews were filled to overflowing with cult members, reporters, police officers, and spectators. The room was thick with noise as Richards and I took our places at the large wooden prosecutor's table. We began to review our notes when a sudden hush began to make its way through the crowd as correctional officers escorted Arvin into the room. I looked up from my notes to see Arvin watching me. He smiled and curiously waved his hand, which was shackled to his waist, as he shuffled to his assigned seat. Without thinking, I awkwardly waved back. Throughout the subsequent commotion, I noticed Arvin staring at me. With his hands still shackled, he motioned for me to come to him. I assumed he wanted to talk, so I asked the corrections officer for permission to do so. The officer approved and walked me to him.

"How did you fare last night, Arvin?" I asked.

"Quite well considering the circumstances" he said. "Mike, what can I do to help you with your investigation? I've already confessed to everything. What else can I do?"

"I appreciate that," I said. "Because you confessed, the children will not have to testify against you. Arvin, I am planning to arrest a number of your followers for similar crimes. I'd like to you encourage them to come in and also confess so that we don't have to make the children testify. Can you do that?"

Again, he smiled that detestable grin and said, "I'll do my best." Moments later, the bailiff brought the court to order, and I quickly returned to my seat as the arraignment began.

Arvin rose and stood next to his attorney as the court read the charges. One by one, he was given the chance to respond.

I held my breath as the judge asked, "How do you plead?"

"Not guilty."

Of course, I was disappointed, but I recognized that it was the right move for him. It was a strategic move by the defense in order to look for weaknesses in the investigation before the actual trial. I was sure they would be dissecting the taped confession in hopes of having Arvin's statements thrown out. It seemed to be their only chance of sparing him from prison. Now my biggest concern was whether the judge would keep Arvin locked up in jail until his trial or release him on his own recognizance.

As the judge announced the trial date, Arvin's attorney requested that he be released from jail. "Arvin will need to assist us in preparing his defense, Your Honor," he said. "We'd request that he be allowed to return home so that we can begin preparing for trial."

The judge listened closely as Arvin's attorney declared his client was not a flight risk.

"If you'll remember, Arvin turned himself into police so that this misunderstanding could be resolved."

What? We had just driven 600 miles roundtrip to pick up this guy who already fled the city! What would prevent him from fleeing again? Richards countered.

"Your Honor, Arvin fled Ogden on or near the day of the raid. He admitted he was traveling around Arizona looking for a place to live. I worry he will take off again. Also, the defendant simply cannot be allowed to return to the neighborhood of the children he's accused of victimizing."

The judge sat motionless as he read over the facts of the case and Arvin's criminal record. After several minutes, he looked up over his glasses and soberly released him on his own recognizance. *Unbelievable!* The judge did, however, agree that Arvin would need to make arrangements to live outside the victims' neighborhood. He ordered Adult Probation and Parole agents to monitor him closely until his trial. We were relieved he was ordered to wear an ankle bracelet to monitor his movements as part of the release agreement. He was ordered to home confinement and I would have to live with that.

As we left the courtroom, Richards stopped me.

"What did Arvin want to talk to you about?" he asked.

"He asked if there were anything he could do to help with the investigation. I told him he could ask the others to confess as well."

"Fat chance of that happening." said Richards.

With that, I headed off to meet with the social workers at the Children's Justice Center as a hive of reporters swarmed Richards.

I arrived at the center shortly after lunch, and the social workers and I gathered around a large conference room table to discuss the interviews. They told me they had accumulated a batch of new evidence, and the children were becoming more comfortable with each passing day.

We now had 11 suspects who were responsible for more than 700 sexual assaults against children. In addition to those pending arrests, the list of additional charges against other members of the cult was growing. These charges were lower class felonies, but they all dealt with child victimization.

The social workers reported the children had made statements that substantiated Erin's claims of Carla selling sex to a man in Logan using children from the group. During the interviews, they also discovered that Carla had made the same arrangements on more than one occasion with another man at a hotel in Ogden. Here, Carla had taken her own daughter to engage in sex with the man while she watched. She told the children, "When we are in Arvin's presence, we do whatever sexual things he wants us to do, but when we are away from him, we are in charge."

One crucial piece of information came from Carla's daughter. She remembered the names of the two men, and I was able to locate the man in Logan through property ownership and rental records. I then subpoenaed the Ogden hotel records to find the other man. Fortunately, each of these men admitted to the assaults and described how Carla orchestrated the encounters and participated in them as well. Their confessions corroborated what the victims had reported earlier. Within a few days, they were both arrested and booked into jail.

When I left the meeting, I decided to take a detour and drive through the Northwood Subdivision once more on my way back to the office. I really didn't have an agenda; I just wanted to look around. The yards looked as pristine as they had before the raid but were unusually quiet. I half expected Arvin to pull into his residence, outfitted with a new ankle bracelet. Even though he'd been ordered to stay away, I wouldn't have been surprised to see him there. I pulled my unmarked car to the side of the street, stopped, and sat. I noticed the curtains in one of the home's upstairs window being closed. I was being monitored. I hoped whoever saw me would somehow get word to Arvin that I was hanging around. Maybe knowing that would make him a little paranoid. Perhaps it would motivate him to mind his p's and q's.

I remained in the neighborhood for about an hour before driving back to my office, arriving there in the late afternoon. As I unlocked my office door, I noticed a message taped to it. The handwriting belonged to our office receptionist, and it read, "You need to call this number today... about Arvin." I peeled the message from the door and headed to her desk.

"It's from a local stripper who wants to talk about the Zion Society," she said.

It took me several days before I could reach the caller. When we finally connected, she identified herself as Marli. She told me she'd seen Arvin in the news a few days earlier and needed to talk to me. She invited me to meet her at a nightclub. I suggested we meet in my office instead, and we set up an appointment for the next day.

The following day, I interviewed Marli in my office. She came across to me as very confident; as someone who could not be pushed around. In a throaty voice she began by saying she had become acquainted with Carla and three other women from the cult a year earlier. "One night these women came into the nightclub where I was working," she said. "They sat down at a table and I noticed them watching me dance. After a few minutes, they kind of gravitated toward me and started stuffing dollar bills into my clothing as I danced. I didn't think much about it, but some of the other dancers whispered to me that they were uncomfortable with the way the women were watching me. I told them that as long as they keep tipping me, I'll keep dancing for them. When I finished my set, Carla followed me to my dressing room and asked if I gave lessons. She told me the women would pay me to come to her home and teach them how to dance erotically. I thought it might be fun and agreed to do it."

Marli went on to explain that over the next four months, she met with the women every Sunday morning for exotic dance lessons. In exchange for her instruction, she was given custom made lingerie as a payment. Little did Marli know at the time, the group had targeted her as a possible recruit into the cult. They had systematically been grooming her for membership in the Zion Society.

"One day Carla asked me to stay late so I could meet Arvin," she said. "He started teaching some kind of weird belief system called The Sexual Way of Life. Then he asked me to join their group. I told him I thought the whole thing sounded really stupid. Arvin got angry and told me I was not invited back. When I asked him why he said, 'because you are not sexually attractive when you are not spiritually attractive. Unless you rise up in your spiritual level immediately, you cannot join our group.'"

Stopping her story, Marli laughed and sarcastically added, "I was so disappointed."

Marli said, that unbeknownst to Arvin, she secretly continued to give Carla and the girls dance instruction. In fact, her relationship with Carla became very close.

When we finished our conversation, Marli said she was willing to testify if needed. She added, "I remember asking why the young girls would come in from time to time and wondered if they were being exposed to sexual things. I didn't do anything about it though. If they were hurting the young girls, I will do anything I can to help you."

I began preparations to speak with Carla and I asked Lucas to join me in the interview.

The next day, I invited Carla to my office under the pretense that we would be discussing her daughter and the assaults we were aware of. Carla knew that Arvin had already confessed to sexually assaulting her daughter, and we hoped this would be enough motivation to get her to come to the meeting. At this point, we were uncertain whether Arvin was sincere in his commitment to have his followers confess their crimes. There was a possibility that he might have used his courtroom offer as part of some overarching scheme to help his own case. Along with his defense team, Arvin could be planning to discredit Carla's daughter's testimony, effectively getting him off the hook. If that were his plan, it didn't have much likelihood of success unless he could also get his confession thrown out. Either way, we would need to be ready for whatever direction this interview took.

We planned to build a foundation about the group's philosophy. We would introduce, albeit superficially, the evidence we uncovered of sustained abuse on the children. We'd then share our knowledge that Carla's daughter was among the children who had been abused. From there, we'd become more focused on Carla's participation in the assaults, ultimately ending with Arvin's confession, implicating Carla. Our trump card would be the confessions of the two men who also placed Carla at the center of the assaults.

Instead of carrying out our plan, however, we spent most of the time just listening. Carla sat down and immediately began confessing. She spewed her own version of what had happened. I stopped her at one point and asked if she had been in contact with Arvin. She said she was in regular contact with him and that she told him she was going to come in and confess. I pressed harder.

"Did Arvin instruct you to confess, or is this something you feel you need to do?"

She dodged my question and answered with what seemed to be a rehearsed statement.

"I want to spare my daughter from having to testify. I did those things to her."

We now had enough information to file multiple sex abuse charges against her, and she was booked into jail.

Over the weeks that followed, this pattern was repeated, day after day. One by one, the remaining suspected women were contacted, and nearly all of them dutifully came into my office and confessed to the crimes they were accused of. Many had their lawyers with them. Some contacted legal counsel after they were booked into jail. All of these women were arrested and booked into the jail or ordered to appear before a judge to face formal charges. They were then arraigned on their charges and were entered into the criminal justice system.

20

Seeking Justice

Now that the perpetrators were booked into jail, our focus shifted to prosecuting them. In all, we had arrested and charged the self-proclaimed leader, one adult male cult member, and nine adult female members of the cult, all with child sexual abuse crimes. Besides Arvin's, we were aware of at least two additional Sister Councils. The adult male cult member who was charged, was the head of one of the Sister Councils. Another male in charge of the other Sister Council was not charged with crimes because no children came forth with allegations against him. Additionally, we charged the two men outside the group for serious felony child sexual assaults.

. . .

I pulled a chair up to Richard's desk and waited as he read over the case documents. His pencil tapped a steady rhythm in between his notations. He was now focused on Erin. Although she hadn't yet been arrested, we had sufficient evidence to charge her with multiple counts of sexual exploitation of children. Despite the fact that she'd come forward to expose the cult and its abusers, I still had questions regarding her motivations for confessing. Besides wanting to stop the cult's practices and rescue the children, did Erin anticipate receiving leniency for her crimes? The fact was that we might never have found out about the cult's practices, or ultimately Arvin's serial rapes had she remained silent. When she confessed to her involvement in the group, she fully realized she could be charged with these crimes herself.

Richards finally spoke up, "It's not uncommon for prosecutors to 'cut a deal' with a criminal in order to get a more serious offender off the streets. We could charge Erin for multiple counts of sexual exploitation of a minor but what purpose would it serve? If we charged her, she would most likely choose not to cooperate, which could cripple our case. Her testimony is crucial to our prosecution. Let's make sure she knows that we're not going to charge her for any crimes she's already confessed to."

The decision was made to give Erin immunity in exchange for her testimony against the more serious perpetrators. In the end, however, her testimony wasn't as damaging to the defendants as the testimony of the child victims.

In an effort to manage the cases more effectively, Richards decided to forego any further arrests for the time being. This would allow him and the other prosecutors ample time to prepare the cases for trial. Because we had obtained confessions in many of the cases, we anticipated that most of the charges would be negotiated. We charged each offender with a substantial number of counts but recognized that piling on more charges wouldn't necessarily bring longer sentences. In each case, the court was aware that there were many other counts that could have been filed. Ultimately, the most compelling reason for minimizing the number of counts each offender was charged with was to spare the children from having to testify and relive the trauma of the assault. We hoped most of the defendants would take this direction, but we had to prepare for anything. There was still a great deal of work to be done on the cases that were now pending in the courts. At the same time, we opened more investigations on eight other cult members.

While all of this was happening, the Juvenile Court dropped a bomb on us by deciding that the children should be released from protective custody and returned to their parents. Although this was obviously a welcomed reunion for most of the children who undoubtedly missed their parents and siblings, it would be a huge impediment in our ability to uncover more criminal acts to which the children had been subjected.

Just as we predicted, as soon as the children were released to their parents, members of the cult hired attorneys who fought our efforts for any additional interviews. The uncovering of any new information about additional crimes slowed to a snail's pace. Also, not surprisingly, parents began downplaying the sexual assaults and warned the children to remain silent about what had happened to them.

Over the next two years, the cases slowly played out as each defendant moved through the court system. Appearances were made, and pleas were entered. Most defendants demanded a preliminary hearing. All charges filed against the defendants were felonies, placing the burden on us to prove to the court that enough probable cause existed to support each charge. The judge had to believe the crime was committed and that the defendant was responsible for committing it.

To our relief, the judges sided with the prosecution on each charge. They found that the state had provided sufficient probable cause in support of each charge.

As each case wound its way through the preliminary hearings, we realized the children were being subjected to repeated questioning and cross-examinations. This situation meant they had to relive the assaults they endured over and over again since most of the victims were abused by each of the twelve defendants.

In one hearing, one of the female defendants had been charged with four counts of aggravated sexual abuse. When her attorney began questioning the victim, he became harsh and insensitive with the young child. He challenged and badgered the young girl to the extreme. The victim bravely held her ground and repeatedly testified she had been abused hundreds of times.

The defendant was bound over for trial and the courtroom was cleared. I happened by a reporter who was interviewing the defense attorney. The reporter asked, "Do you think you were too tough on the child?" To which the attorney said, "I didn't consider it tough at all; she hasn't seen anything yet."

The child's stepmother was standing next to me and overheard the comments.

"They forget these are just kids," she said painfully.

One defendant did escape prosecution because the prosecution's young witness simply could not testify. The little six-year-old child was so emotionally traumatized, the mental health providers recommended we dismiss the case. This was an agonizing reminder of how unfair the laws were in regard to the manner and method of dealing with child victims in court. I could sense Richards was troubled with the system. He remarked that more needed to be done to protect the children while ensuring due process. In the end, we all agreed the welfare of this child was more important than prosecuting her abuser, and we withdrew the charge. We were furious this man got away with serious sex crimes. The damage he inflicted on this innocent child would last a lifetime, and he walked away free, touting his innocence, even though he was on record confessing to the assaults. The remaining 12 defendants were bound over for trial.

With each of the remaining charges, we presented a strong case backed with testimony from the victim, testimony that proved convincing and damning. Each child's testimony was backed up and verified by the professional assessment of social workers and psychologists. In some of the cases, we also put independent witness testimony on the record to support the victim's allegations. Some of our witnesses were children from the cult who testified they observed the assaults from hidden locations within the homes, undetected. Other witnesses testified how they were forced to participate in the assaults. In many of the cases, we introduced medical examination findings that were consistent with the injuries expected in this type of sexual abuse.

The strongest pieces of evidence were the testimonies of the victims which were corroborated by most of the defendants' own confessions.

As the time for the trials approached, plea negotiations intensified, and several deals were struck. As each arrangement was agreed upon, the prosecution and defense requested pretrial conferences seeking the approval of the judge, who could refuse to accept the negotiation. Richards orchestrated a number of brilliant moves at this time, leveraging the overwhelming volume of uncharged cases that we had against each defendant. Months earlier, at the time of the arraignments, he decided to file charges on only the most egregious cases. Like a shrewd player in a game of poker, he kept a few good cards in his deck. Reserving the tactic for just the right moment, Richards could threaten to "throw the book" at the defendants and charge them with many more counts if necessary. He could instead offer not to file any additional charges if the defendants accepted plea agreements. Richards' "take it or leave it" proposition worked flawlessly.

While defendants mulled over their limited choices, we examined the impact that the slow-moving cases were having on the victims. We were confident the children were facing ever-mounting levels of stress. As each case neared its trial date, we found ourselves asking how much longer we could expect these children to remain within this terrible cycle.

Case by case, the preliminary hearing dates arrived. The prosecution would appear in the courtroom with all witnesses, evidence, and court documents. Then, in what appeared to be an effort to avoid the embarrassment of the enormous amount of evidence getting out to the public, every defendant changed their position and pled guilty to the charges. They hoped it would help them minimize the cult's actions in the public eye. All of the preparation and hard work paid off, and every single charge resulted in a conviction. Best of all was the fact that the children were spared from having to testify another time.

Most of the defendants were sentenced to one to 15-year prison terms. In a few cases, the court decided to suspend the defendant's prison sentence if the offender agreed to complete a 90-day work release program and promised to pay restitution. The defendant had to agree to discontinue any contact with other group members and enter an Intensive Supervision Program. I joined in the outrage of many of the victims who wondered how that judgement could be considered fair punishment for child sexual exploitation and child sexual abuse. Although Arvin's legal wife, Alice, was an enabler in the abuses, she was not charged with any crime.

After Carla was made aware of the charges lodged against her by her daughter, I confronted her one day in court.

"How are you doing, Carla?"

"I am fine," was her stoic reply. Then she began to volunteer an explanation for some of her actions, exposing her deranged logic. She told me there was a reason she had arranged for her daughter to be abused by the two men outside the cult.

"Some of the things my daughter told you aren't completely correct," she said. "She has the facts correct, but you do not understand what my intent was. Looking back on it I can see how wrong I was, but I thought I was doing the right thing by getting her interested in other men. You see, she had become quite attached to Arvin and I felt this was the only way to end the relationship."

Carla was convicted of sexual exploitation of a child, aggravated sexual abuse of a child, and sodomy on a child. Each charge held a minimum mandatory sentence of five years to life.

Arvin was found guilty of two counts of sodomy on a child and two counts of sexual abuse of a child. As he stood before the judge to be sentenced, Arvin surprised the court with one more request. While sitting at the defense table, he whispered something to his attorney. The attorney stood and addressed the judge. "Your Honor, the defendant requests that the investigator stand alongside him for his sentencing." I was taken aback and glanced at the judge half hoping the request would be denied. Oddly, the judge granted it, "If the investigator would like."

I tried to quickly assess the request as I hesitatingly walked into the well of the courtroom. Suddenly, the tearful look on Arvin's face in that diner the day he surrendered flashed through my mind. His words thanking me for treating him kindly rang in my ears. Was that all a manipulation by the master con man or had he been sincere? It didn't matter. We had gotten his confession and that was all we cared about. OK Arvin, I thought. I'm willing to play along. Perhaps he thought the judge would be more lenient seeing the lead investigator standing with him. Little did he know, I had my own motivations. I knew his followers who had not yet been charged were sitting in the courtroom, and I wanted them to trust me and also plead guilty. As I slowly passed by Richards sitting at the prosecution table, we gave each other inquisitive looks. I moved across the room to the defense table and stood alongside Arvin. He turned toward me, nodded his head appreciatively, and whispered, "Thank you," as the judge issued his sentence.

The judge was required under Utah's minimum mandatory sentencing laws, to send Arvin to the Utah State Prison for no less than ten years to life. The judge handed down a sentence of 20 years to life. Arvin appeared shocked and confused; the color drained from his face. It seemed he was expecting a much lighter sentence. He turned to address his attorneys but was not given a chance to speak to anyone. Correctional officers placed him in handcuffs and led him from the courtroom. The following day he entered the Utah State Prison. While there, he appealed the sentence but lost. He remained incarcerated until the day he died.

In all, there were an astounding 746 counts of sexual crimes against the children. Arvin was responsible for 390 of those assaults. Carla faced 113 counts, while the remaining eight women in the Sister Council were responsible for 226 counts, and the two non-cult men were responsible for 17. We had planned to charge additional cult members, both men and women, with additional sexual abuse charges, but the court system was taking too long. After two years, we chose to stop the prosecutions in order to spare the children from further trauma.

Along with many others, Jeff Peterson had watched the case proceed through the courts.

"I'd like to see Arvin hang," he said. "But I'll settle for life imprisonment. He needs to be kept away from society. He's very eloquent, very persuasive, very charismatic. He woos women away and breaks up families. Arvin is a pervert."[1]

21

Prison Antics

When the dust settled, convicted cult members sat impatiently in jails and prisons across the state. Most tried to convince prison social workers and the parole board of their repentant hearts, presenting themselves as victims who had been fooled by Arvin's charisma. I felt the women confessed to their crimes in hopes the court would look on them with leniency. It was easier to think of a man committing such horrible crimes than to think of a woman doing so, or even more unbelievable, a mother in Carla's case. Their ploy worked to some degree. Most of the women were released within a year. I was frustrated with a system that would allow such short periods of incarceration for such serious offenses. I didn't see the fairness of permitting these criminals to return to some sense of normality, knowing their victims, the children, would likely suffer for much of their lives.

As Arvin and Carla sat facing long sentences, the remaining cult members were busy redefining themselves. Those who had been convicted and released from prison were court-ordered to stay away from each other. They were under the supervision of Adult Probation and Parole and were not allowed to return to the group. One by one,

Arvin's followers left Ogden. Some went to live with relatives or friends, but several, astoundingly, found other cults to join. Faced with mounting bills and fewer group members to provide income, cult members started selling off the group's homes while they awaited guidance from their imprisoned leaders.

While the cult collapsed, social workers had to make arrangements for the children of those members who had not been charged to return to their homes, the very homes of sympathizers of the abusers. A special fund had been created several years earlier by the Utah Legislature and the Utah Office for Victims of Crime. Victims could apply for the funds to help them pay for mental health counseling and medical bills. In a few of the cases, the judge ordered counseling for adults as part of the release agreement to get their children back. None took the counseling, but they got their children back anyway. All of the children were offered free counseling, but their parents made sure the did not receive it.

Cult members who had not been arrested began making weekly trips to visit Arvin at the Utah State Prison and Carla at the Utah State Women's Correctional Facility. Members also talked to the two by phone as often as the Department of Corrections would allow. When they were given permission to talk, both Arvin and Carla gave instructions. During their prison orientation, the inmates were informed that any telephone conversation, other than those with attorneys, could be recorded. Arvin and Carla either forgot that tidbit of information or didn't care about it. They feverishly tried to rebuild the cult from inside the prison facilities while correctional officers monitored their conversations.

Every three to six months, I would ask for a transcript of the prison phone calls. Many of the early calls to Arvin and Carla centered around their distress regarding the length of their prison sentences. Some calls expressed hope that their attorneys would uncover a trial mistake or find some kind of error in the investigation that might lead to an overturned conviction.

In June of 1992, I was given a transcript that intrigued me. It was a conversation Arvin had with one of the cult members. "Gather as much dirt on Mike King as possible," he said. "Don't talk too much to the press. Sick ----- on King's tactics and techniques. It is time for the other side of the story to be told." He concluded by saying, "God is going to take a hand in things."

Several days later, Arvin's daughter-in-law called Arvin to inform him that his son was having conversations with the press. "Tell him no more TV interviews. Bite it off!" Arvin bellowed. He then cautioned her to make sure everyone knew that phone calls into the prison were recorded. Before hanging up, Arvin declared who the presiding male member of the group should be in his absence. Interestingly, he did not choose a family member.

As time went on, divisions began to appear between members of the group. Arvin and Carla were not allowed to communicate with each other, and while Arvin was giving his orders, Carla claimed to be receiving revelations of her own. She told one cult member about a dream she had where she was in a deep fog. When the fog lifted, she realized she was drinking baby formula. As the dream progressed, she graduated from formula to whole milk. She was then approached by a man who said to her, "Get rid of the milk, you are ready for meat."

Carla went on to say that she started seeing stars. "There are some big changes coming. The [prison] warden is interested in our group and ideas. The door is wide open for better things." Carla then instructed the members to get $500 and put it on her prison account. She didn't explain what it was for but ended the call, saying, "I know it will upset the houses a little, but come up with it in a couple of days."

As Carla's delusions intensified, her demands on the group increased. In public, she was telling the press and members of her estranged family that she had forsaken the doctrines of the Zion Society, and denounced Arvin. Behind closed cell doors, she was proselytizing the same perverted message that sent her to prison. Transcripts showed that she was telling cult members she had, in fact, converted an inmate to their belief system. She instructed one cult member to meet the ex-con on her release date and help her get into a home that didn't have any ties to the group. Before she ended the conversation, she said, "Get $200 from the group. Be very low key. Make sure [the ex-con] doesn't see the whole group. Bring her along slowly. Help her with schooling." Before she hung up, she said, "I'm learning how to play the game in prison."

I was surprised, but not shocked, at how much control Arvin and Carla still maintained over cult members from their jail cells. At times I wondered if they were becoming delusional, and at other times I would marvel at their detailed plans. On one occasion, Arvin devised a scheme to have all the group members feign repentance and try to get back in good standing with the Latter-day Saint faith.

Eventually, Arvin and Carla started talking in code during their phone calls to protect their plans. It created an entertaining pastime for me as I worked on decoding their conversations. Each of the cult members was given a code name. I discovered one name in particular belonged to one of the child victims. Carla instructed several of the women in the cult to find this victim and start gathering information on her.

Their concern was that I had reached out to this victim after social service workers had picked her up before the raid. This ingenious young girl was Amber. She had snuck out of the child's dormitory and entered Arvin's house while no one was watching to use the only phone in the cult. She called CPS in New Mexico where she had once lived and reported herself as a runaway. In turn, CPS in New Mexico contacted Arizona CPS, where Amber was last known to have been enrolled in school. Arizona CPS came to Ogden, found Amber in the cult, and returned her to foster care in Arizona.

Appalled, I listened as Carla said, "She could do a lot of damage to us. Expose her drug problem, etcetera, so we can shoot her down. King thinks he has a witness. She must have talked."

Once I learned about Amber, I traveled to Arizona to interview her. We were still prosecuting the cases, and Carla was convinced the child would tell all, expose other adults, and potentially add more cases against her. What Carla didn't know was that Amber refused to talk. The girl's only comment to me was, "I am more afraid of God than I am of you."

As the long months of trials dragged on, cult members didn't know that I had changed employment. I was now working for the Utah Attorney General, investigating ritual child sexual abuse. My experiences with the Zion Society had prepared me for the task of analyzing, understanding, and investigating ritual crime. While I wasn't a fan of the title "ritual crime," after pursuing Arvin and the other predators who followed him, I realized it was a correct term. The term, "ritual crime," was a popular and sensational description of the crimes we were charged with investigating. In reality, these crimes were fundamentally physical, emotional, or sexual abuse crimes. The ritualistic nature of the offense is what made them aggravated crimes. The offender's method of controlling the victim using repetitive behaviors is what actually made them ritualistic.

I was surprised at the attention the newly formed crime unit was getting. Ninety percent of Utah citizens believed that ritualistic child sexual abuse was occurring in the state.[1] It troubled me that so many people erroneously defined "ritual" as "satanic," inferring that the crimes were connected with satanism. It actually wasn't true of most of these crimes. Rituals are any sequence of activities involving gestures, words, action, or objects performed in a sequestered place and according to a set sequence.[2] The idea of using a deity as a control method to force others into sexual victimization has been repeated by many offenders. In reality, few of these crimes rise to the level of an organized cult, let alone a satanic cult. It is repetitive controlling behaviors where a deity, threats of injury to family pets or siblings, and so forth are used to control the victims, gain compliance, and ensure the victim's silence that makes the crime ritualistic.

Although I was no longer involved in the Zion Society cult case, I continued to monitor Arvin, Carla, and other cult members. In 1995, as the trials were winding down, the Ritual Crime Task Force was concluded, and I took on a new assignment. I was assigned to look into the major polygamist groups in the state to gain a better understanding of them.

Polygamy is no stranger in Utah. For many years, law enforcement tended to turn a blind eye to the practice. Prosecutions were just not successful. Unmarried adults living together were not breaking laws, but married adults claiming more than one spouse were. What law enforcement was interested in were allegations of child brides and welfare fraud. At times, I longed for the days when I was buying and selling stolen vehicles as part of the STING Task Force. In hindsight, it seemed I was destined to work ritualistic crimes.

22

And So It Goes...

As the years passed, I rarely thought about the Zion Society case unless something forced me to. A trip to central Utah was one of those times. Several years had gone by, and Richards and I found ourselves working together again, this time in the Utah Attorney General's Office. It was autumn of 1998 when the two of us drove through a small community in central Utah on some official AG business.

As we drove down what could barely be called Main Street, I saw the name of a polygamist church printed above the doorway of an old, red, two-story building. As we passed, I noticed the front door was open and thought this would be a good opportunity to learn about this particular group. I flipped a U-turn in my undercover car and pulled in front of the building. Opening the car door, I asked, "Want to come with me?"

Richards shrugged his shoulders. "Why not?"

Once inside, we saw that the building looked empty. There was what appeared to be a reception area, but it wasn't staffed. We called out, "Hello?" but there was no answer. Across the room, a long set of stairs led to the second floor. I could hear a man's voice talking quietly from the floor above. I motioned for Richards to follow me up the stairs. At the top of the staircase stood a large office. Seated with his back to the office doorway, a man appeared to be speaking on a phone. I knocked on the doorframe, and the man jumped. Leaping to his feet, he mumbled, "I'll call you back," as he hung up the phone and turned to face us.

"I'm sorry we startled you, sir. We couldn't find anyone downstairs."

"You scared me half to death," he said, chuckling. "Can I help you?"

"We're investigating your church and would like to know more about your beliefs," I said.

The words just slipped out but were absolutely true. We were investigating him and his church.

"Welcome. Sit down and let's talk," he said.

For the next two hours, the man who identified himself as the leader of the polygamous group taught us about his church and beliefs. Our interaction with him was friendly and very engaging. He concluded by giving us a book of scripture and inviting us to come back another time. He said that he welcomed the chance to continue the conversation, and we scheduled another meeting for a couple of weeks later.

I kept the appointment, but Richards was unable to accompany me. He suggested that I take a highway patrol trooper from the state's intelligence center. The trooper and I had previously collaborated on several cases involving polygamists. He looked concerned when I told him the man we would be visiting was under the assumption that we were interested in joining his church.

"We're going to be preached to today, sergeant," I said. "Look interested and inspired."

As we pulled up in front of the church on Main Street, we were met by the group leader and two other men. After exchanging a short greeting, we all walked toward the sanctuary where a group of seven or eight men were standing by, ready to inspire and instruct us. Along the way, the church leader asked if we'd like to stay for lunch. At the same moment the trooper began to say, "No," I said, "We'd love to."

The man laughed and said, "You're in for a treat. One of my wives is a fabulous cook."

As we sat through nearly three hours of indoctrination, I found myself thinking back to the grooming tactics Arvin and his followers employed as they tried to convert people to their way of thinking. For the first time, I felt I was experiencing a little of what they had. Listening to this man was grueling, and I was relieved when it finally came to an end. When he finished speaking, he invited us to walk with him the short distance to his home for lunch.

When we arrived at the home, we were greeted by two friendly women in long-sleeved, ankle-length dresses standing on the doorstep. The man introduced them as his wives. Then a third woman stepped through the door.

As soon as she saw me, she screamed, "It's that damnable devil Mike King!"

The group leader froze.

I smiled and said, "Hello Stephanie, I wondered where you moved to." Yes, she had been one of the women I put in prison several years earlier as a member of the Zion Society.

As the leader tried to gain his composure, another woman stepped out of the home.

When I greeted her by name, she glared at me with contempt. She had also been a member of the Zion Society cult that I'd arrested.

We were abruptly ordered from the property with angry expletives. As we drove away, I wondered what they had prepared for lunch. I was sure it was better than the gas station hotdog we ate instead.

From time to time, during the years that followed, I continued to have run-ins with former members of the Zion Society. It was disheartening to think that these people we had hoped would change simply chose to join a different cult. In a few cases, former group members somehow found each other after getting off parole. Together, they proceeded to move into other polygamist communities.

Carla was released after nine years, but Arvin remained incarcerated for the rest of his life. Several years before he died, I visited him in his prison cell. We ate lasagna together and talked about his experiences in the penitentiary. He wondered about my career, and we spoke about his confession. That day he told me something I have never forgotten.

"I would have never confessed to you, Mike," he said, "except you treated me like a human being."

I asked Arvin if he would be willing to speak to a group of about 500 police investigators from across the state. I told him I was leading a program called UTAP, the Utah criminal Tracking and Analysis Project. UTAP was designed to look at unsolved homicides, missing persons, unidentified bodies and serial sexual crimes. I shared where my career had taken me, including the opportunity I'd been given to be trained by criminal profilers. I also explained that I eventually became an instructor to law enforcement officers across the country.

"Arvin," I said. "I can teach people about criminal behavior and how to be a profiler. That's what I've done in my career. What I can't do is tell them how a criminal thinks, but you can. Would you be willing to answer their questions?"

He was hooked. If profiling taught me anything, it taught me that past behavior is predictive of future behavior. I was offering Arvin an audience, something he hadn't had for over ten years. He jumped at the chance, and we set up the training, titled "Ritual Crime and Polygamy."

On the day of the event, Arvin was transported to a conference center in Salt Lake City where 500 police officers eagerly awaited the chance to learn from this ritualistic sex offender. Not surprisingly, Arvin spoke for over an hour without any notes. For ten long years, he had been sitting in a jail cell, only communicating with other inmates and periodic visitors. Now, here he was, addressing law enforcement officers, and he was composed and well prepared. He was in his element. The instructor. The professor. He tried his hardest to be likable and charismatic, which was a challenge given his audience. His performance gave me a glimpse into his personality and his ability to persuade. One of my former profiling colleagues, Greg Cooper, also spoke to the all-police audience.

He said to the officers, "Can you imagine how you'd act if you were put in front of 500 inmates and asked to speak and answer their questions? This guy remained cool and collected as he spoke to this group."

Arvin told the officers that he was responsible for all the things he was charged with but asked them to understand his righteous motivations and feelings. He spoke about his ability to debate.

"Debating is not about coming to an understanding of truth. It is about winning," Arvin said.

As I sat listening, I envisioned him teaching his misaligned doctrine to his followers. That said it all. It's about winning. He admitted to the officers that he hadn't accepted the offer for counseling in the prison because he disagreed with the curriculum and felt it was a waste of time in his circumstance.

Arvin paused only once when one of the officers asked, "What do you think about child abusers?"

He responded, "I think they are loathsome. It's unfortunate and it shouldn't occur."

Shocked by the answer, the officer retorted, "Aren't you an abuser?"

Arvin answered confidently, "You could look at it that way, I suppose. Any other questions?"

Before ending the training session, I asked Arvin if he'd like to make any other comment. He said he would, but only about polygamist groups in general. He stiffened slightly, sat up straight in his chair, and in an authoritative voice began to lecture.

"You're going to be facing an awful lot of these communities. If we see properly the economic situation which is shaping up in the world, we may be in for an economic squeeze in this country before it's over with. And what does that mean in relation to groups [like mine]? People tend to band together when you've got socio-economic problems. You think you've got groups now, if this thing tightens... wait'll ya see what happens. Well, are all of these people going to turn into child abusers? Of course not. [If] you go out with the attitude of law enforcement, that anybody that's banding together as a group has some form

of skullduggery going on, you may find that you're wasting an awful lot of time. But on the other hand, if you take down the barriers and build some rapport with the people, talk to them... get to know them. Let's use a little common sense and try and break down the barriers of isolation and get to know people a little better. Maybe then we can prevent an awful lot of these problems from arising. And I say that without trying to make it as an excuse of any kind or an explanation other than contributing factors to myself. Thanks."

Arvin died in prison on August 10, 2009. After serving her sentence, Carla moved to a rural community and lives near three other former Zion Society cult members. Four cult members are known to have joined other polygamist groups. The remaining cult members have moved off the radar screen; their whereabouts or doings are unknown to me.

23
Survivors

July 18, 2018

I turned on the computer in my home office, as I did every day, when an unfamiliar email popped up in my inbox. The subject line was, "Re: Zion Society," and came from a girl named Amber.

"Mr. King, I hope you remember me. Would you be willing to talk and help me sort out some of my memories from the Zion Society? I would really appreciate it."

It had been 28 years since I had last spoken with Amber. Just seeing her name in the message brought back a flood of memories. I had retired from law enforcement several years earlier and was now working for an international mapping software company out of southern California. My first instinct was to block her emails. The very thought of reliving the investigation into the Zion Society's child sex abuse cult made my stomach clench. It had been one of the most disturbing and difficult cases I'd investigated in my entire career. I had effectively buried it away when the last predator was sentenced to prison.

I did not answer the email. Within days, almost as if orchestrated, I received another email from a different victim of the same cult.

Andrea's email was asking to talk about the cult as well. It read in part, "I struggled every day with debilitating memories of my abuse."

I was surprised how vivid my memory was of her being escorted to an awaiting Child Protective Services' van those many years ago.

For several days, I pondered the requests. Each time I sat down at my computer to work, I re-read their emails. Finally, I responded.

"Thank you for the email. I don't think I would be able to provide you any additional insight into the case. It was so many years ago. I wish you the very best as you seek answers."

Although I had dodged an emotional bullet, my decision haunted me for months. I couldn't get these victims off my mind. Who was I to tell them what was in their best interest? They had endured hundreds of rapes and sexual assaults. And now, they asked for my help and I turned them down. I felt a heavy burden of guilt for having done so but couldn't imagine how I could possibly help them. After all, I was a retired detective, not a therapist.

A few weeks later, I received a phone call from my long-time friend, Reed Richards.

"Hi Mike, it's Reed. The Victim's Rights Council would like you and me to do a review of the Zion Society case. What do you think?"

I have never been one to believe in coincidences. Nonetheless, I told him, "No thanks." I didn't want to talk about the case anymore.

Many months passed, and one day while in the storage room of our basement, I glanced up at a top shelf and saw the boxes marked "Zion Society." I pulled them down and contemplated burning all my files once and for all, but I just couldn't do it. Instead, I shuffled through the many documents and began to question my responses.

True to his persistent nature, Richards called again with the same request. For some reason, this time, it felt right. I said I would do it.

Fueled with a new sense of purpose, I needed to know answers to many questions: How did this middle-aged pedophile convince so many people that he spoke for God? How did his cult go undetected for years? How did he convince members to engage in child sex abuse? What happened to the victims? Where did the perpetrators end up?

What did we learn from the investigative and court processes? And finally, what could we have done better?

I was able to connect with Andrea right away and we scheduled a video conference call.

. . .

May 29, 2020

As I adjusted the camera and microphone on my computer, I wondered if Andrea was as nervous about our pending video conference call as I was. It had been nearly 30 years since we last spoke. I thought of how much had transpired over my life during that time and I was hoping her story would be filled with happiness and success. I heard the chime on my computer and Andrea's face appeared on the screen. The memory of her staring angrily at me during the raid came flooding back.

"Hi, Mr. King. You look much different than I remember."

I laughed. "I'm much older. You look great Andrea. I can vividly see your 16-year-old image in that 44-year-old face. How are you doing?"

Andrea began to explain how hard it had been for her to get through life.

"I want you to know that I hated you for 15 years, Mike. And then something clicked inside. I realized you had actually saved me. You were the 'parent' that rescued me when my own parents would not. Thank you for being that for me in my life. But I still felt abandoned because no one helped me get counseling."

She explained that she had experienced deep depression in her twenties and blamed it on severe internal anger. Shutting down became her coping mechanism. She lacked any self-confidence and had received no guidance in her life.

"I felt like a failure. I eventually sought out a therapist, which was helpful," she added.

She said she had struggled with relationships, bouncing from one to another. Once she left the group, she became very promiscuous. "That's all I knew to do," she said.

To make matters worse, she said her parents never apologized for the things that happened to her. She expressed to me that she herself didn't ever want to have children and she blames her mother for that.

At age thirty, Andrea said she mustered enough confidence to give college a try. She worked menial jobs and scraped enough money together to pay for one semester at the University of California at Berkley. She worked tirelessly at her schooling and even demanded help from the disability office on campus to provide her with least ten tutors during the first semester. Much to Andrea's surprise, her efforts caught the attention of her professors, and the university offered her a full-ride scholarship. She graduated with honors and is now pursuing a master's degree in social work.

It hadn't been easy, but this girl who spent her childhood in a deviant cult where she was told what and how to think, was now thinking on her own, and it was empowering. I was enormously proud of her.

Andrea said that although she had tried to bury her past, it kept resurfacing, along with nagging questions.

"Why didn't the courts force my parents to get me counseling?" she asked. "By the time I was old enough to make my own decisions, I was already in a bad place. If state money was available for counseling, why didn't I know about it when I turned 18?"

These were all excellent questions, but I had no answers to them.

Following my conversation with Andrea, I began a quest to locate as many victims of the cult as I could. After much searching, I was fortunate to locate several who agreed to talk to me. Each had a heart-rending story of struggles and insurmountable challenges they had to overcome in their lives.

. . .

For all of the women I spoke with, the first few years after the raid were among the most difficult in their young lives. Before the raid, they sensed their lifestyle was wrong, but they believed everything their parents and spiritual guardians were telling them. What child wouldn't? They were taught that God approved of children being sexually active. Andrea expressed the sentiments of all the victims when she explained, "We didn't know it was wrong until you told us it was."

Many of the victims were mere children at the time of the raid. The entire ordeal placed severe trauma on their young psyches. Most were forced to struggle with their trauma on their own.

Kami, Erin's daughter, especially touched me as she described the pain she had gone through. She explained, "Sexual abuse literally cracks a child into a million pieces. I spent all of my life until 2009, when my abuser died, living in horrible fear that he would get out of prison and come find me and kill me for getting him busted. I spoke out as a tiny child against monsters, and I lived many, many years in absolute terror, fearing my abuser would come after me. I felt so alone with so many questions."

While other teenagers were going to ballgames and school dances, Kami spent her teenage years trying to learn about evil, sick people and their mindset. She wanted to be able to recognize the warning signs. She also had a deep-seated need to understand that the abuse wasn't her fault. She shared some of the same questions as Andrea. "Why didn't anyone care? Why didn't anyone stop it and save us? And why did no one care afterward?"

Once in a while, Kami drives past the city courthouse where justice was handed down to the abusers. "To this day, it does not feel like justice," she said.

I learned that after the hearings, many of the victims' parents pretended to leave the group and reject its teachings. To show they were willing to return to a normal lifestyle, they enrolled their children in the public-school system. The victims soon realized they had fallen behind the other students academically. The only subject they could keep up in, if not excel at, was reading. They were excellent readers, as long as the text was scripture. They had been forced to read scriptures every day and most of the day. Understanding meaning and content in other subjects was difficult for them. Math, science, and social studies were completely foreign concepts to them. Most of the children failed to advance through the school grades, and many simply dropped out of school.

The cultural shock of assimilating into society was more than most of these girls could handle. They felt self-conscious, out of place, and intimidated, which resulted in them withdrawing even further from the society they were trying to fit into. If the victims did develop a friendship with children outside the cult, it was short-lived as they got to know each other. Often, their parents prevented them from having friends over or going out with friends, a residual control tactic from their days in the cult.

As the girls matured, education became a priority to some. Dawn was 10 years old at the time of the raid. She was one of Arvin's granddaughters. She faced huge challenges because her parents, not surprisingly, denied or downplayed the terrible things she had gone through. After the raid, she felt like she lived in a bubble of denial for years, sweeping the past under a rug. Her parents taught her and her siblings to put on blinders and just move past the Zion Society experience. In adulthood, Dawn recognized the difficulty she was having in dealing with life and sought out counseling. She also came to realize that getting an education would empower her and help her gain confidence. Eventually, she, like Andrea, attended college and received a bachelor's degree in anthropology and psychology.

Because of her insecurities about leaving her children with babysitters, Kami has not been able to go to school or get employment. She and her husband courageously struggle to keep a roof over their family's head. Kami's biggest priority now is her young children. She is determined to be the best mother she can be—something she feels the cult denied her mother.

Following the raid, the older girls chose to move into their own apartments. With little education, they struggled to support themselves with menial jobs. Hourly wages were the norm for them. Some utilized skills they had developed in the cult and found jobs as seamstresses and cooks.

Amber escaped the cult before the raid. She fled to Arizona and then bounced from foster home to foster home before going out on her own. She began living the tenuous life her parents had lived before they'd joined the cult, a transient from-hand-to-mouth existence consisting of sleeping in cars and eating leftovers from the garbage. Before long, she took a job working as a stripper in a Phoenix club. "Acceptance from others is a powerful high," she said. "I wanted it." Amber leveraged the only thing she knew considering her third-grade education, sexuality. She utilized the extensive instruction she had received from the exotic dancers who had trained the Zion Society girls to strip. Stripping gave her the attention she craved, and she boasted that she was very good at it.

"I decided I wanted to be of the world, a part of the world, not in a bubble. I wanted to know what was really going on in the world as a defiance to the small world we had lived in," she said.

Eventually Amber realized she needed an education to improve her situation. Although she tried to pass the GED test three separate times, she just couldn't get past the math section. Amber had always been resourceful, and she came up with a plan. She asked a friend who just happened to look a lot like her, to use Amber's ID and take the test for her. Amber now proudly claims her GED on job applications. Today she is a creative writer and entertainer. She has a wicked sense of humor and works as a comedian, where she uses humor to help her deal with her past.

Annessa, who was eleven during the raid, worked tirelessly to become a successful real estate agent in Ogden. She told me about an experience she had one day when her job took her to the Northwood subdivision. She said she fell apart and began a conversation with herself, "I'm a grown-up. This shouldn't be affecting me like this."

Natalie was seven years old when the cult was raided. She was the child of one of the prominent men in the cult, and her mother was the man's "spiritual wife." The man did not want to admit he fathered Natalie with a woman who was not his legal wife. Natalie was told her father had died, and she was instructed to refer to her biological father, as her uncle.

I was impressed with how perceptive and articulate Natalie was as we spoke. She has found much success as a popular romance novelist, writing under a pseudonym.

Laura, as one of the older victims during the raid, was not treated as a victim. She was 18 years of age, and she was considered an adult. Although she had been abused for more than four years before turning 18, she was overlooked by Child Protective Services and hadn't been interviewed. Instead of focusing on high school during her teenage years, she was required to work minimum wage jobs to support Arvin and the cult. Through remarkable hard work and determination, she has since advanced in the professional world to become a very successful business manager in Ogden. It would take nearly 30 years for the state to recognize her as a victim, rather than a participating adult in the group. With the support of Richards, and the current county Attorney, Christopher F. Allred, the State of Utah classified her as a victim of the Zion Society cult, clearing up an existing official police report that listed her differently.

Promiscuity was a challenge for many of the victims when they ventured out on their own. They were left alone to learn the mores of society regarding sexuality and relationships. Some mistakenly used lessons they learned in the group to keep a boy interested in them. The girls felt a sense of power and control over boys knowing they could use sex for attention. Some experimented with sex and had difficulty finding committed relationships.

"I didn't know much, but I sure knew how to please a man or woman," was the sentiment expressed by many.

Both same-sex and opposite-sex relationships were common for a couple of victims. Understandably, the victims have struggled with relationships. Many hid their past from boyfriends that would later become husbands. Through the first years of marriage, unhealthy behaviors demanded they expose their past in order to preserve their families. Some have been fortunate to find understanding companions who help them work through their difficult history. Some marriages have failed. All have sought counseling at one time or another.

Several of the women are now in committed relationships and are devoted to raising healthy and happy children. Kami said it well, "My children come first; they need me to not be consumed with my demons." Painfully, she looks back on her past, wishing there had been some type of program to help her get through the horrors she endured during her childhood.

Not surprisingly, many victims of the cult retain negative feelings regarding religion. Some try to be objective, differentiating between the cult that only professed to be a real religion and legitimate religious organizations. Others want nothing to do with any type of religion; some harbor a hatred for them in general. All, of course, retain deep-seated anger for the cult, the leader, and the adults who stood back and allowed the practices to take place.

. . .

From time to time, I would be troubled by memories of the horrible Zion Society case and the end result of the court system's judgements. I kept reminding myself that there was nothing more we could have done. We had done everything we were trained to do, maybe more. We did our very best to remove the victims from the predators who tormented them, albeit a shorter duration than we had hoped. We had arrested and convicted 12 people and ensured Arvin would die in prison. We took advantage of the victim's reparations fund to ensure there was adequate money to pay for victim counseling. In many of the cases we even secured court orders that required the parents to guarantee the counseling was completed. But it didn't happen, and the victims received no counseling. The system failed these children and young women.

What we didn't do, we couldn't do. There wasn't a mechanism in place to follow through with the victims' progress. Certainly, social service case workers would have maintained some oversight, but the victims moved away and were otherwise forgotten as other cases cropped up. Also, we didn't realize how seriously non-conforming the victims' parents would be. They refused to honor the court's demands as long as they believed God not only permitted but actually encouraged the assaults. Regrettably, there was little we were able to do at the time. Still, perhaps we should have kept trying.

As I mulled over the challenges the women faced now, they seemed to boil down to three primary issues: mental health counseling, education, and finding a way to help other victims. A plan was coming into view.

My first call was to the most knowledgeable person I knew in victim support, the former county attorney Reed Richards. Having been through the entire case from beginning to end, Richards was completely onboard. As we discussed the problem, we decided to bring the Director of the Utah Office for Victims of Crime into the discussion. Gary Scheller started serving victims in 1992 as a court-appointed special advocate for child victims. Six years later, he became a reparations officer in the state's office for victims of crime. Scheller was ultimately appointed director in 2012. If anyone could figure out a way to help the Zion Society victims, he could. Gary was excited to help and asked for a few days to work out some details.

I then reached out to Dr. Brad Mortensen, president of Weber State University in Ogden. President Mortensen had served in WSU's administration for over a decade and was named president in 2018. He willingly accepted my call and listened intently as I outlined the background of the case and my hope that he could identify some pathways to help the women get an education. He promised his support and also asked for a few days to think about it.

. . .

Timing is everything, and the timing seemed right. It was July 2020, and the women asked for a group meeting where they could see one another on a video conference. I was surprised to learn the survivors had not been in touch with each other for nearly thirty years. They had all gone their separate ways and tried to put the past behind them. After several emails and phone calls, we came up with a date to connect. This meeting would turn out to be one of the most interesting and meaningful reunions I've ever been a part of.

On the designated day, Richards, myself, and survivors of the Zion Society began what would become a three-hour video conference call. As each woman's image appeared on the screen, there were screams of joy as the childhood playmates saw each other for the first time in decades. They laughed. They cried. And they shared extraordinary stories. At times they spoke of horrifying events and repeated abuses. Now finally, they had a support system of victims who understood each other. Andrea summed up the experience when she said, "It seems that being more visible would only serve to help others and hopefully help myself. It's felt like a heavy burden all these years, dragging around a secret that's rarely talked about. Let's talk about it."

After a couple of hours of listening to the women reminisce, Richards spoke to them about our decision thirty years ago to stop prosecuting cases. He reminded them that the trials lasted almost two years as we worked through the twelve defendants we had charged. With each preliminary hearing and trial, the children were required to testify. It had worried us. In fact, it sickened us to think about the subtle re-victimization the children couldn't help but suffer as they were forced to relive the assaults. For that reason, we decided that having the predatory leaders and the major offenders behind bars seemed to be enough. We knew there were others who could have gone to jail, but we purposely considered the cost to the children of putting the offenders there. In the end, we determined that we needed to stop in order to protect the victims.

I invited two other guests to join the call. The first was Melanie Scarlet from the Utah Office for Victims of Crime. I watched the faces of the survivors as she announced that the state would welcome the chance to help all of them with counseling. She provided each a single point of contact who would know of the commitment and help them get reimbursement for mental health counseling. We all became emotional as the women expressed their gratitude and utter astonishment. To my surprise the state also agreed to pay for counseling for the victims who were now living out of state and another who would soon be departing overseas. It was a remarkable and rewarding moment.

It was then President Mortensen's turn to speak to the survivors. He expressed his gratitude in being trusted with their stories. As he spoke of their individual triumphs over their childhoods, he promised them that the university would help them get an education if they desired it. He cautioned them that it would require hard work on their part, but whether they chose to pursue a GED or a PhD, he'd help. His commitment included assigning a single point of contact to meet with each woman and determine what steps would be required to meet her educational needs. Once they obtained their GED, the women would receive assistance in finding grants or scholarships to help their dream of an education come true. The call fell silent. The women seemed to be in disbelief.

The efforts many have gone through in an effort to assist victims of this horrible cult are commendable and uplifting (albeit late in coming). These victims' individual triumphs cannot be overstated. They have overcome insurmountable odds and continue to forge ahead through their challenges.

Those mentioned in this book, however, were not the only victims of this insidious cult and its leader. Unfortunately, several other child victims chose to put their experiences behind them and move on without resolution.

And then there was Erin. She delivered a baby boy while living in the cult and was able to escape with both her children. Although she admitted to having been a perpetrator, she too, in her own way, was a victim of this devious cult. And like the other victims, she faced enormous challenges through her later life as well. She struggled with many of the same pains the young victims described. Because she was never charged with any crime, she wasn't offered any counseling or assistance.

In reality, there were many victims of this heinous cult. Men, women, and children were manipulated, coerced, and deceived by the cult's deviant leader. Some continue to be deceived, maintaining their belief in the self-proclaimed prophet. Others have moved on to follow other polygamous groups or charismatic leaders. They continue in their extremism, almost as if it were inbred in them. Others have simply blended back into society, and their whereabouts and feelings about their cult experience are unknown.

Amber Dawn Lee

Andrea Lithgow

Natalie Root

Dawn

Annessa

Laura

Kami

Final Thoughts

A "cultic relationship" is one in which a person intentionally induces others to become totally or nearly totally dependent on him or her for almost all major life decisions and inculcates in these followers a belief that he or she has some special talent, gift, or knowledge...

There are many differences between a religion and a cult, but the major difference is that of the ultimate goal. Established religions and altruistic movements are focused outward – they attempt to better the lives of members and often, nonmembers. They make altruistic contributions. Cults serve their own purposes, which are the purposes of the cult leader, their energies are focused inward rather than outward.

Singer, M.T. 2003. *Cults in our Midst,*
The Continuing Fight Against the Hidden Menace

The pervasive question of those involved in the Zion Society investigation was how anyone could have been manipulated into joining the repulsive cult. It might be surprising to understand that under the right circumstances normal, average people can be susceptible to joining a cult. Research indicates approximately two-thirds of cult members are psychologically healthy people who come from normal families and only five to six percent of cult members demonstrate major psychological problems prior to joining a cult.[1]

Most of the people who joined the Zion Society cult seemed to be cut from the same cloth. They were religious zealots and extremists whose objective in life was to live in a community of like-minded people who possessed what they believed was a higher level of spirituality than others. They believed God would (or they wanted God to) direct them in every decision they needed to make, no matter how trivial. They desired a leader to outline and guide their lives. Followers saw themselves as elite and favored in God's sight. Perfection was stressed in every aspect of their lives. Several members were looking for a group that practiced their long-held beliefs in polygamy or "plural marriage." Some families had lived in other polygamist communities in the past. Extremism convinced the members that the end of the world was near, and they would be among the few who survived. Intense preparation became their focus. Paranoia of the "outside world" compelled the group to accumulate and store weapons.

Dr. Janja Lalich, emeritus professor of Sociology at California State University, Chico, is an expert in cult research. She developed an important list of "social-structural, social-psychological, and interpersonal behavioral patterns" commonly found in cult environments. The Zion Society displayed nearly every characteristic associated with cults.

1. The group is elitist, claiming a special exalted status for itself, its leader(s), and its members (e.g., the leader is considered the Messiah, a special being, an avatar – or the group and/or the leaders is on a special mission to save humanity).

As with other destructive cults, the Zion Society had a self-appointed leader who claimed to have special knowledge denied others. He was a self-proclaimed prophet who pretended to have revelations from God. He deceived and manipulated the religious zealots by using scriptural language as well as biblical writings in his "heavenly" instructions. Cult members were enamored with his knowledge of the scriptures, his belief in polygamy, and his charismatic personality. He promised his followers they would receive "heavenly exaltation" if they heeded his teachings—that they would obtain "a fulness of joy and be one in all things."

2. The group displays excessively zealous and unquestioning commitment to its leader, and (whether he is alive or dead) regards his belief system, ideology, and practices as the truth, the law.

His followers regarded Arvin as their prophet, and some even referred to him as a god. Children were taught to refer to him as their "king." Cult members believed every dictate from him and showed their admiration and devotion to him through strict obedience. Arvin was gifted in persuasion, and he required and received a complete commitment and obedience from his followers. He was controlling and domineering in a soft-spoken sort of way. He wore a façade of humility that endeared his followers to him, convincing them of his claims to divine authority.

3. The leadership dictates, sometimes in great detail, how members should think, act, and feel (e.g., members must get permission to date, change jobs or marry – or leaders prescribe what to wear, where to live, whether to have children, how to discipline children, and so forth).

Cult members were instructed in every aspect of their life from the spiritual to the mundane, such as what to believe, wear, eat, and weigh. They were required to give their money to Arvin, who would decide how it would be distributed. By turning their lives over to Arvin, his followers were promised a less complicated life with simple solutions to everyday challenges. They were taught to rely on Arvin and heavenly help for even the most ordinary day-to-day decisions. The mindset of the group members was that they preferred to be told what to do and how to think, rather than be responsible for their choices. Arvin shrewdly granted members responsibilities, which gave them a sense of purpose and invested them in the group more thoroughly.

4. *Questioning, doubt, and dissent are discouraged or even punished.*

Arvin's abominable practices within the group began subtly, and members followed their leader without question. The slightest criticism or inquiry regarding any of Arvin's or Carla's directives meant being ostracized and humiliated by the group.

5. *The group is preoccupied with bringing in new members.*

Because the Zion Society cult of polygamous minded people started out small, recruiting and fundraising became both long- and short-term goals of the group. Arvin was the expert at recruiting and retaining cult members. With his background in debate, he was well versed in researching. Whether he researched other cults or studied psychology or just experimented with manipulation until he found the method that worked best for him is unclear. It is clear that he was successful in growing the group to over 100 members and he trained the cult members to become experts in identifying and recruiting new members.

Through the Search and Separate program, the women in the group were trained to look for other women who were facing difficulty in their lives. Strippers, recent divorcees, unwed mothers and women fleeing troubled marriages were prime targets. On the website, 'Working Psychology' Dr. Kelton Rhoads says, "There appears to be no reliable personality factor that predicts cult membership. However, certain situational elements make people more vulnerable to cult recruitment, and they include: loneliness, depression, and uncertainty about how to proceed. These situations create the desire for quick, simple solutions. Cults provide a myriad of "solutions" which are more importantly accompanied by structure, authority, and close social contacts—

elements people want, need, and which most of us take for granted in the course of our everyday lives."[2]

Erin was the perfect profile of the kind of person the group recruited. She was trying to escape a failing marriage but felt locked into it because of her pregnancy and the fact that she believed she had no way to support herself. Once she was identified, the group systematically encircled her with friendship and offered her free housing, childcare, and food. She felt loved, understood, and unjudged by the group members. Dr. Singer states, "It is not one type of person who gets enmeshed with cults, but rather a person who has a combination of factors occurring nearly simultaneously. I have found that two conditions make an individual especially vulnerable to cult recruiting: being depressed and being in between important affiliations. We are especially prone to the cults' kind of influence when we're not engaged in a meaningful personal relationship, job, educational or training program, or some other life involvement."[3]

6. Subservience to the leader or group requires members to cut ties with family and friends, and radically alter the personal goals and activities they had before joining the group.

Once Erin accepted help from the group, she was systematically groomed into accepting and complying with the cult's beliefs. She became dependent on the group for her needs. To help create this group dependency, Arvin separated new recruits from family and friends. Erin was not allowed to talk to her husband or other family members. She was also required to get rid of any remembrances of her past life such as wedding rings, photos, and other mementos. She was soon under the control of the cult. Children in the cult were separated from their parents in order to facilitate brainwashing and illegal acts. They were only allowed to see their parents a couple of times a year. The children were also separated from their siblings and were not allowed to have a best friend in the cult. The children were constantly moved from one house to another in order to break up friendships. Emotional connections were not allowed. In fact, children were not allowed to have emotions. If they had a problem, they were expected to figure out a solution on their own. The adults offered no support.

7. Members are expected to devote inordinate amounts of time to the group and group-related activities.

Life inside the cult was strictly managed. Some adults held jobs that helped with finances. At the same time, the children stayed home and were kept on strict schedules doing chores, studying scriptures, sewing, gardening, meditating, training in sexual seduction, and working on a minimal amount of schoolwork—all under the supervision of the Sister Council.

8. The group is preoccupied with making money.

Women cult members were required to spend an enormous amount of time and effort in the group's business, "Sweet Things," in which they were expected to design and sew women's lingerie to sell. Another strategy the cult used to make money was to target women in struggling marriages. They would entice the women into leaving their husbands and joining the cult. The women would bring their children with them and then extort their husbands out of thousands of dollars in order for fathers to get their children back. Since boys were expendable in the cult, fathers could only negotiate for their sons' return, not their daughters'.

9. Members are encouraged or required to live and/or socialize only with other group members.
10. The group has polarized, us-versus-them mentality.

The adults did not associate with people outside the group unless they were recruiting, and the children were not allowed to play with other children in the neighborhood. Arvin promoted a "black and white" philosophy regarding the outside world. Adults avoided outsiders, and children were taught to fear them. Followers believed they were living in Zion while the rest of the world represented Babylon.

11. The leadership induces feelings of shame and/or guilt in order to influence and control members. Often this is done through peer pressure and subtle forms of persuasion.

Arvin was a master manipulator. He terrified the children by telling them God knew their thoughts and actions, and God would then tell him. He convinced the children he could read minds. The children were fearful of his revelations, not knowing what these revelations might require of them or who they might condemn. Although this so-called prophet and authority on religion and scriptures taught members to pray about everything, he never held any kind of church service with his followers. He only held group meetings to deliver instruction and to reprimand members. This was another mind-controlling maneuver. Members were ostracized by the other members of the group when they weren't compliant. Also, the women and the girls in Arvin's Sister Council were weighed daily and humiliated in front of others if they didn't fall within Arvin's prescribed ideal weight measurements.

12. The group teaches or implies that its supposedly exalted ends justify whatever means it deems necessary. This may result in members participating in behaviors or activities they would have considered reprehensible or unethical before joining the group.

As time went on, Arvin's teachings became more and more perverse. Several followers accepted and even participated in his claims of divine revelation regarding child sex abuse, most notably, Carla, Arvin's second in command, along with his other spiritual wives. Other followers, including parents of the abused children, simply turned a blind eye to the abuse, justifying it with their belief that God had ordained it. They were taught and believed they were living according to a higher law. Arvin used the guise of religion to achieve his fantasies. He convinced his followers that he spoke for God. They accepted Arvin's declarations that God was directing the affairs of his "religion" no matter how abhorrent the teachings and activities became, even to the point of becoming accomplices in abuse.

Dr. Singer describes a cult as "a mirror of what is inside the cult leader. He has no restraints on him. He can make his fantasies and desires come alive in the world he creates around him. He can lead people to do his bidding. He can make the surrounding world really his world. What most cult leaders achieve is akin to the fantasies of a child at play, creating a world with toys and utensils."[4]

In reality, Arvin was no prophet or exalted being but was a narcissistic pedophile. He was a sexual pervert and a con man who masqueraded his cult of perversion under the pretense of religion.

. . .

Many of those adults who joined the Zion Society had been deceived just as Erin had. In some ways, those working on the case felt a sense of pity for them. The brainwashing had been so deep that cult members could not comprehend any other way of life. Afterward, many simply sought out similar groups to continue their lifestyle and deny any wrongdoing. Accepting responsibility for their mistakes would mean enormous guilt and shame for these individuals.

There are many questions regarding Arvin. Although his sexual perversions progressed through his bad choices, were they initially generated by the experiences he had with an aunt when he was a young boy? When did he begin showing signs of narcissism? Did his feelings of superiority begin with his success in school, or did his school success merely contribute to his narcissism? Arvin obviously had mental health issues. Did he have an undiagnosed form of schizophrenia that made him think he was a prophet of God? Did any of his family encourage him to seek help? Were his motivations in creating the cult purely based on his desire to satisfy his sexual perversions? Did he study other cults to learn their methods? Where did Arvin learn to master his manipulation techniques?

Before he died, Arvin demonstrated an unusual insight into the psychology of cult membership when he talked to law enforcement officers from prison. He warned that cult communities thrive during social and economic distress. When most people think of a cult, they envision religious-themed organizations such as the Zion Society. Frighteningly, cult mentality pervades many parts of society. Dr. Singer warns that cults can be cloaked behind many facades that are normally legitimate. Cults can be disguised as restaurants, self-help groups, business-training workshops, prosperity clubs, psychotherapy clinics, diet plans, political parties, campus activities, and martial arts centers.[5]

For the children who grew up in the cult, their reality was a complete aberration. They would be destined to face struggles and challenges throughout their lives. Dr. Singer explains, "Cult children have no opportunity to observe the compromising, negotiating, and meeting on middle ground demonstrated in ordinary families. They do not see people resolving disputes or adjusting to the wants and desires of others, the trade-offs that are so central to learning how to play, work, and live in a family or in groups that have been socialized in democratic ways…As a result, anxious-dependent personality traits can be built into cult children's developing character. These children don't have an earlier personality or knowledge of the world to build upon when they come out of the cult. Compared to other children, many children raised in isolated cults emerge with restricted learning, fewer skills, and below average socialization."[6]

The children from the Zion Society would experience depression, abnormal fears, trust issues, perfectionism, and self-doubt. Those who were fortunate enough to find a support system, whether in a partner, friend, or professional, consider themselves very lucky.

. . .

Raiding the cult had an immediate short-term impact on the children. As far as we know, the cult's sexual abuse of the children ended. But the victims will probably carry the scars of the abuse throughout their lives.

Reed Richards, former Weber County Attorney and former Chief Deputy Attorney General for the State of Utah, explains that as ugly as this case was, there were positive long-term benefits that came from it.

The Children's Justice Center system was in its infancy at the time of the raid. The lessons learned from the time the children were picked up in the raid through their experience in the center and ultimately the Criminal Justice system, helped to refine and improve the services provided in the centers throughout Utah and the nation. There are now 26 Children's Justice Centers in Utah and hundreds more across the US. This case made it clear Children's Justice Centers should medically examine abused children for forensic evidence and conduct evaluations regarding the welfare of the child. The centers now provide mental evaluations and psychiatric treatment for abused children as needed. The challenges presented by interviewing the Zion Society children made it clear the interview process is much better accomplished by professionals trained in forensic interviewing of children. These professionals are generally not police officers but are forensic interviewers who are skilled at developing a rapport with the children in a less stressful environment, which can generally produce better responses. We learned psychiatric evaluations and continued therapy are an essential part of the recovery process.

He goes on to say, the Zion Society case, and other child sexual abuse cases, provided the impetus and justification for amending the Utah Constitution to provide for the rights of child victims in the criminal justice process. The Utah Constitution now mandates that children be treated with kindness and dignity throughout the justice process. The constitution now allows many of the court hearings to use the statements recorded in the Children's Justice Center instead of requiring children to testify in court. Not having to testify at the preliminary hearing removes one of the most dramatic parts of the prosecution. Generally, children in Utah who have been interviewed at a Children's Justice Center are never required to testify in court. Children and their parents are now, by constitutional provision, provided timely information regarding the case and given the right to provide information to the judge at the time of sentencing and at other stages in the criminal justice process.

Helping victims through the criminal justice process and providing assistance and counseling to help facilitate recovery from the trauma of child abuse is an ongoing process. The victims of the Zion Society cult who have been willing to speak up and advocate for other victims will significantly help the process move forward. They are to be commended for their willingness and their courage.

Notes

Chapter 1
Innocenceproject.org

Chapter 2
1 Schneider, M. (1984) 'Shreeve: Eloquent, skilled, independent', *Ogden Standard-Examiner* 3 Jul
2 Ibid
3 Ancestry.com
4 Schneider, M. (1984) 'Shreeve: Eloquent, skilled, independent', *Ogden Standard-Examiner* 3 Jul
5 The Church of Jesus Christ of Latter-day Saints.org/ essays, 'Plural Marriage in the Church of Jesus Christ of Latter-day Saints (originally published 2014)

Chapter 3
1 Wagner R.G., Baker D. (1984) 'Mysterious group troubles neighborhood'. *Ogden Standard-Examiner* 3 Jul
2 Wagner R.G., Baker D. (1984) 'Neighborhood residents troubled by mysterious group'. *Ogden Standard Examiner* 3 Jul
3 Associated Press (1991) 'Sexual abuse? 9 Children Taken Away' *Salt Lake Tribune*, 3 Aug
4 Wagner R.G., Baker D. (1984) 'Neighborhood residents troubled by mysterious group'. *Ogden Standard Examiner* 3 Jul

Chapter 16
1 Associated Press (1991) 'School Run by Ogden Group Fails to Meet State Standards', *The Salt Lake Tribune* 7 Aug. p.35

Chapter 20
1 *The Salt Lake Tribune* (1991) 'Official Says 10 of Cult's 30 youths were abused', 28 Dec. p. 16.

Chapter 21
1 Henetz, P. (1992) 'Satanic Abuse is Real' *Deseret News*, 17 Jan https://www.deseret.com/1992/1/17/18962594/satanic-abuse-is-real-90-say-br
2 Ritual, Merriam-Webster Dictionary https://www.merriam-webster.com/dictionary/ritual

Final Thoughts
1 Singer, M.T. with Lalich, Janja (2003). Cults in our Midst, The Continuing Fight Against the Hidden Menace. Jossey-Bass, p.17
2 Rhoads, K., (1997) www.workingpsychology.com, Ritual, Merriam-Webster Dictionary
3 Singer, M.T. with Lalich, Janja (2003). Cults in our Midst, The Continuing Fight Against the Hidden Menace. Jossey-Bass, p.20
4 Ibid., 5
5 Ibid., 254
6 Ibid., 258

Bibliography

Associated Press (1991) 'School Run by Ogden Group Fails to Meet State Standards', *The Salt Lake Tribune* 7 Aug. p. 35.

Associated Press (1991) 'Sexual abuse? 9 Children Taken Away' *Salt Lake Tribune*, 3 Aug

Church of Jesus Christ of Latter-day Saints.org/ essays, Plural Marriage in the Church of Jesus Christ of Latter-day Saints (originally published 2014)

Henetz, P. (1992) 'Satanic Abuse is Real' *Deseret News*, 17 Jan https://www.deseret.com/1992/1/17/18962594/satanic-abuse-is-real-90-say-br

Innocenceproject.org

Lalich, J. Characteristics Associated with Cults, Cult Research, http://cultresearch.org/help/characteristics-associated-with-cults/

Rhoads, K., (1997) www.workingpsychology.com,

Ritual, Merriam-Webster Dictionary https://www.merriam-webster.com/dictionary/ritual

The Salt Lake Tribune (1991) 'Official Says 10 of Cult's 30 youths were abused', 28 Dec. p. 16.

Schneider M. (1984) 'Shreeve: Eloquent, Skilled, Independent' *Ogden Standard Examiner*. 3 Jul

Singer, M.T. with Lalich, Janja(2003). *Cults in our Midst, The Continuing Fight Against the Hidden Menace.* Jossey-Bass

Wagner R.G., Baker D. (1984) 'Neighbors describe 'curious' lifestyle. Neighborhood Residents Troubled by Mysterious Group' *Ogden Standard Examiner* 4 Jul

Acknowledgements

This memoir could not have been written without the assistance of many individuals. I thank those who contributed their first-hand experiences: Reed Richards, Dave Lucas, Ron VanDrimmelen, Susan Herzog, Cheryl Naugle, Richard Martin, Ron Van Beekum, Jacquie Van Beekum, Judy Heninger, Marcy V. Korgenski, Mark Acker, Katie Larsen, Bill Van Dyke, Bob Van Dyke, Blaine Clifford, Dave Weloth, Joan Hellstrom and Terrie Lynn McConnell.

I could not have completed this work without the help of my wife, Bonnie, who put in countless hours assisting in the writing and organization of this manuscript. I am also very appreciative of Inge Moore and her expertise in editing.

I'm grateful to Scott Wiser for his skills in design and formatting; and Tyler Cahoon for his artistic contributions.

Most importantly, I can't say enough about the survivors and their contributions. Thank you to these heroes who were brave enough to share their memories: Amber Dawn Lee, Andrea Lithgow, Natalie Root, Annessa, Laura, Dawn, and Kami.

Mike King has worked in the law enforcement field for over 40 years. He received a BA and an MA in Criminal Justice and began his career as a police officer in northern Utah. He became an investigator in the Weber County Attorney's Office and subsequently in the Utah Attorney General's Office where he also served as Chief of Staff. He trained in criminal profiling under FBI Special Agent Gregory Cooper (ret.). He and Cooper were the investigators for the Discovery Channel's Emmy Award winning investigative documentary: Who Killed King Tut? He entered the private sector in 2004 and began working for Environmental Systems Research Institute (Esri) as the global director of emergency communications and fraud. Other books he has authored are: *Who Killed King Tut, Predators: Who They Are and How to Stop Them, Profilers,* and *Jane: A Woman's Determination and the Wild West Frontier.* He and his wife, Bonnie, are the parents of three children and they have four grandchildren.

To inquire about booking Mike King for a speaking engagement, please contact ProfilingEvil.com
An audio and digital edition of this book is also available.
Profiling Evil, LLC

Made in United States
Orlando, FL
27 December 2024

56553461R00128